GRACE

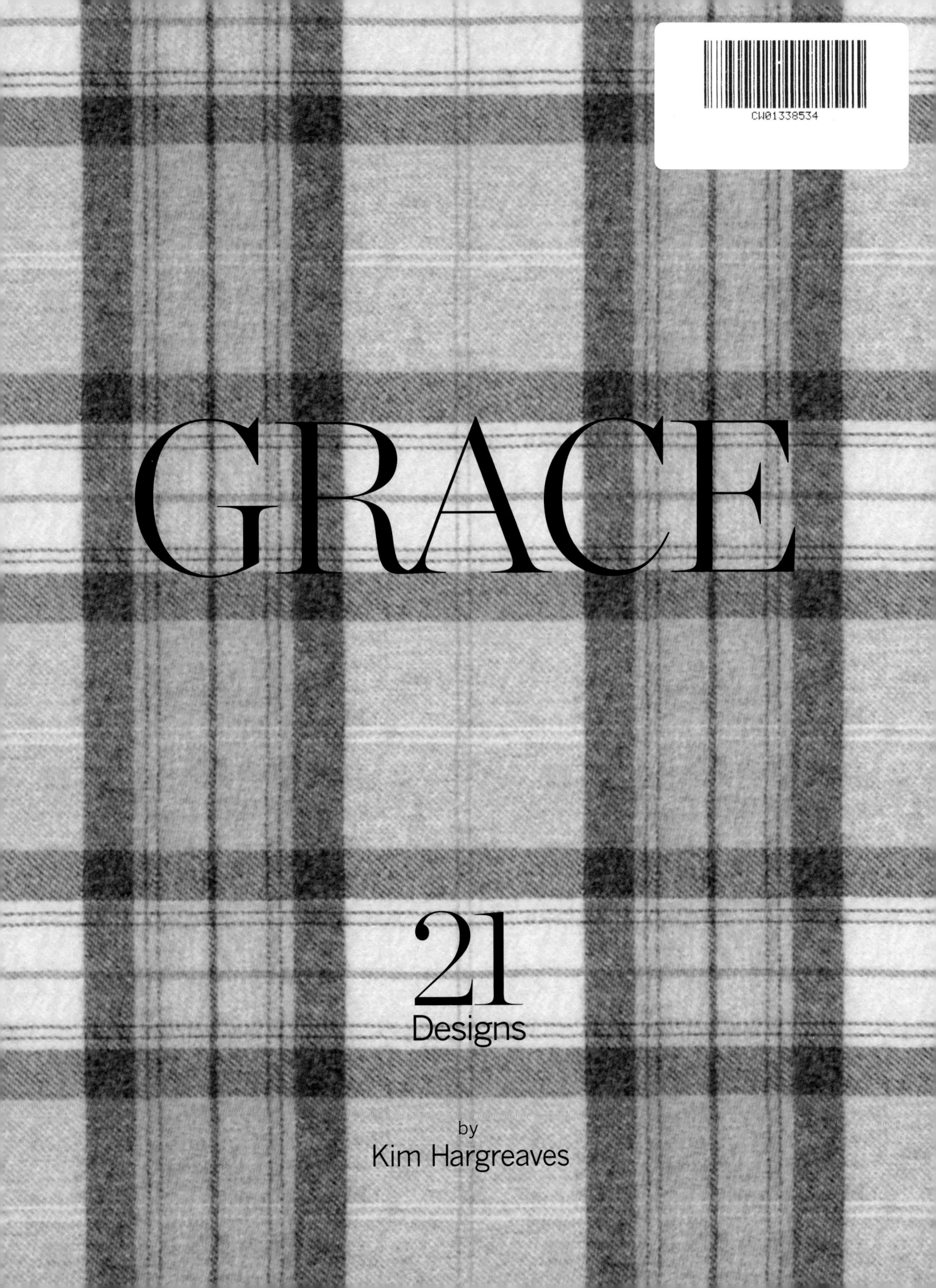

21 Designs

by
Kim Hargreaves

CREDITS

DESIGNS & STYLING
Kim Hargreaves

EDITOR
Kathleen Hargreaves

MODEL
Kristie Stubley

HAIR & MAKE-UP
Diana Fisher

PHOTOGRAPHY & EDITORIAL DESIGN
Graham Watts

LAYOUTS
Angela Lin

PATTERNS
Sue Whiting & Tricia McKenzie

© Copyright Kim Hargreaves 2016. All Rights Reserved.

First published in 2016 by Kim Hargreaves, Intake Cottage, 26 Underbank Old Road, Holmfirth, West Yorkshire, HD9 1EA, England. No part of this book may be reproduced, stored in a retrieval system or transmitted in any form or by any means—electronic, electrostatic, magnetic tape, mechanical, photocopying, scanning, recording or otherwise—without prior permission in writing from the publisher.

British Library Cataloguing in Publication Data.
A catalogue record for this book is available from the British Library.

ISBN-10   1-906487-26-3
ISBN-13   978-1-906487-26-3

CONTENTS

THE DESIGNS   7
Bold monotones give way to softer shades that seamlessly
reflect a backdrop of dramatic moorland & cloud laden skies

THE PATTERNS   56
Find the information needed to complete each design

INFORMATION   94
A guide to help with techniques & finishing touches

INDEX   97

NOT SO & WHITE BLACK

Nothing is as it first appears. Bold monotones give way to softer shades of heather, moss and mist greys that seamlessly reflect a backdrop of dramatic moorland & cloud laden skies. Indoors, where a wistful mood prevails, shelter is offered to graceful garments worked in cosy cables, delicate lace and pretty arans. Silhouettes, whether long and lean, understated and oversized, or simply curve defining, capture the season perfectly.

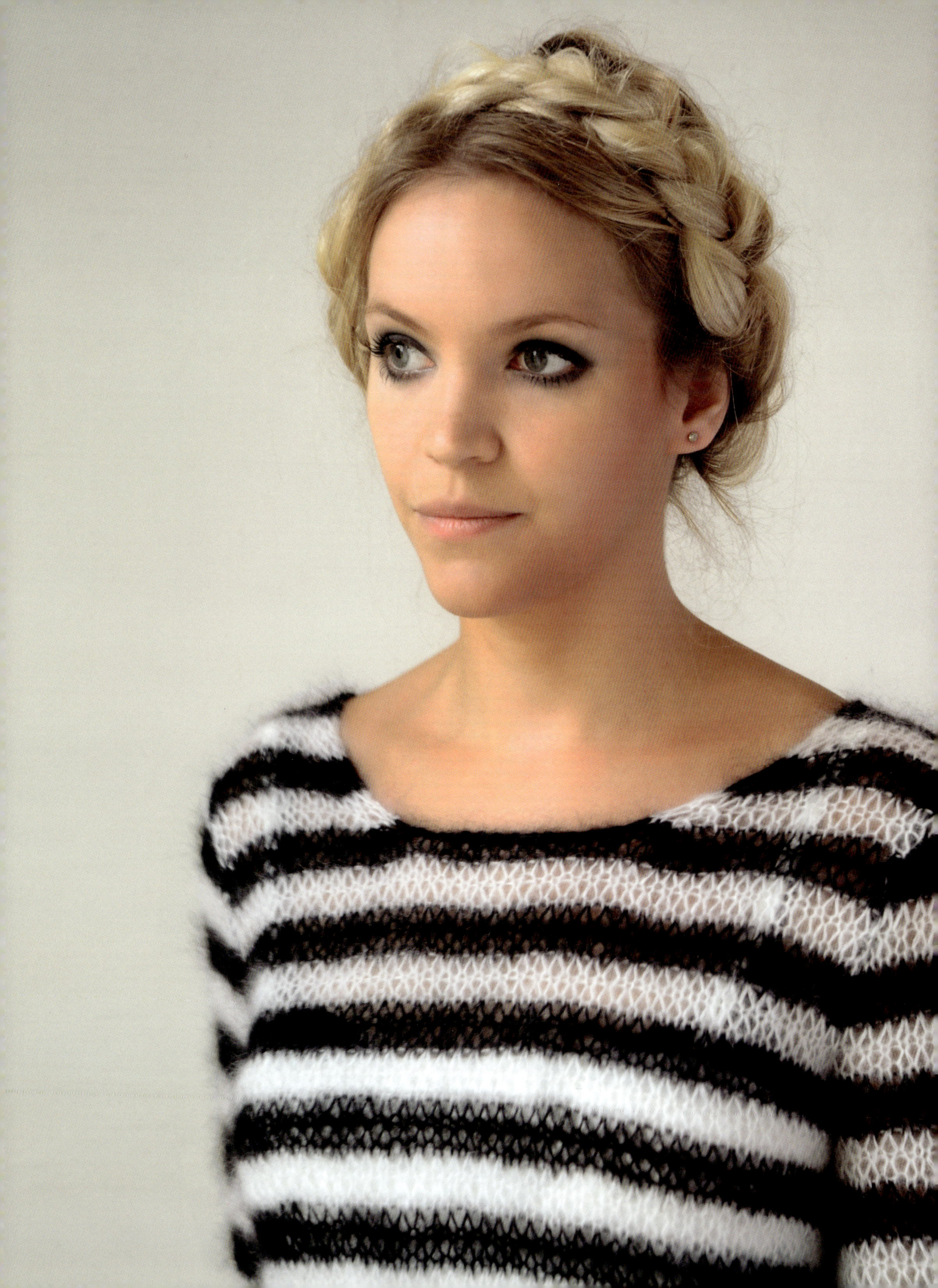

BARRETT – a simply striped sweater in striking black & white

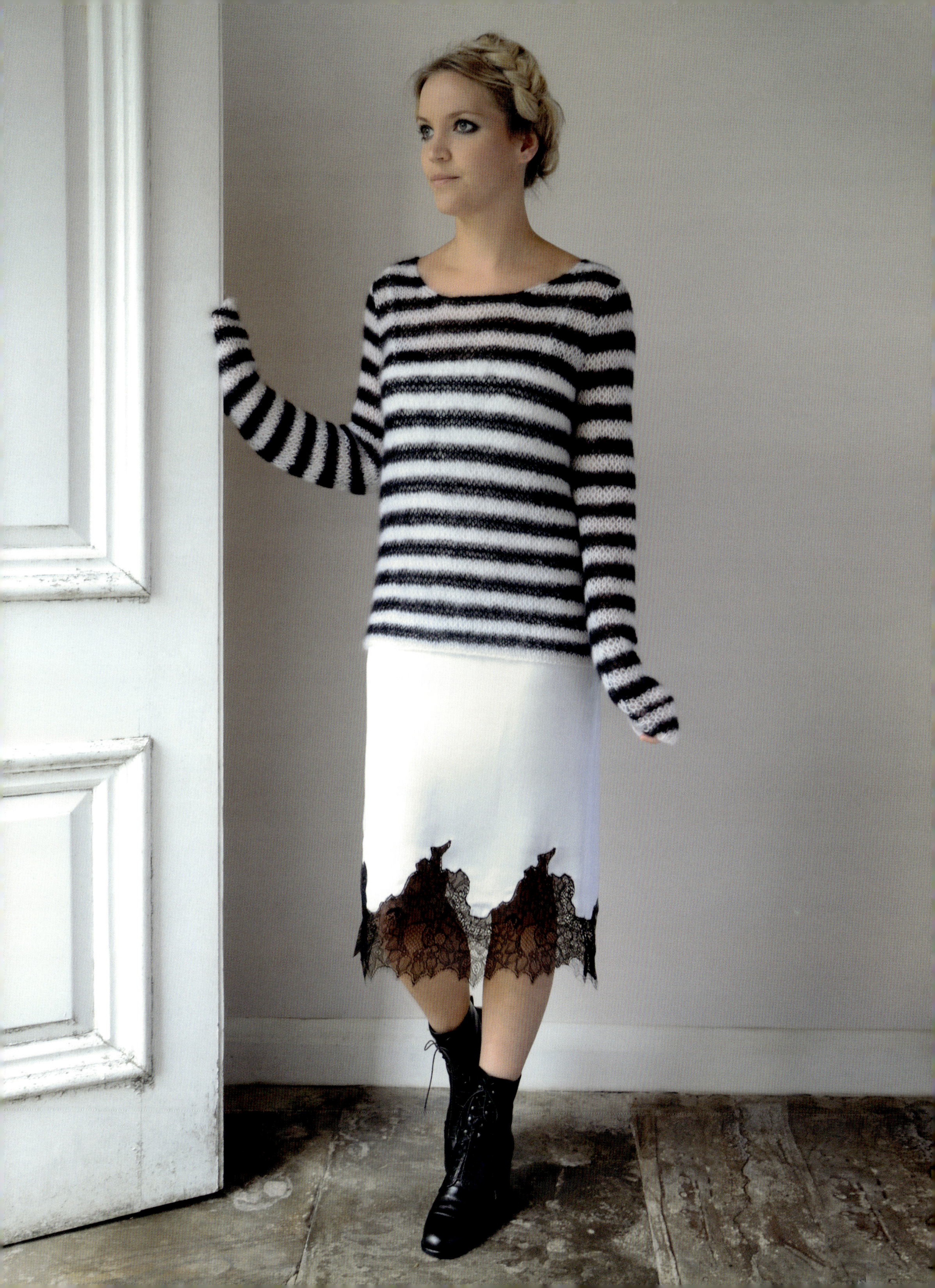

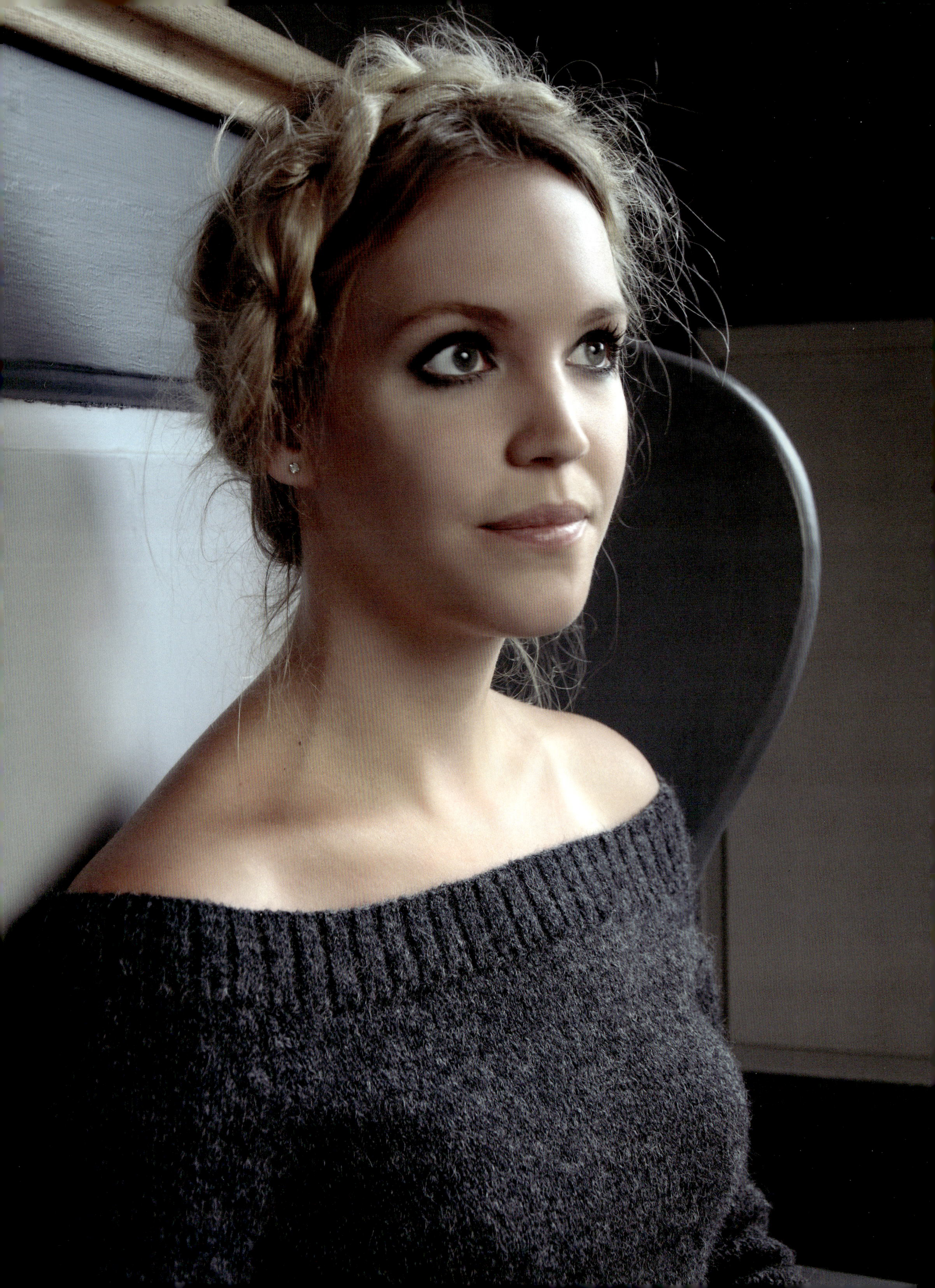

JESS – a fitted off the shoulder sweater with side vents

ADAIR – an understated close-fitting vest with deep side vents

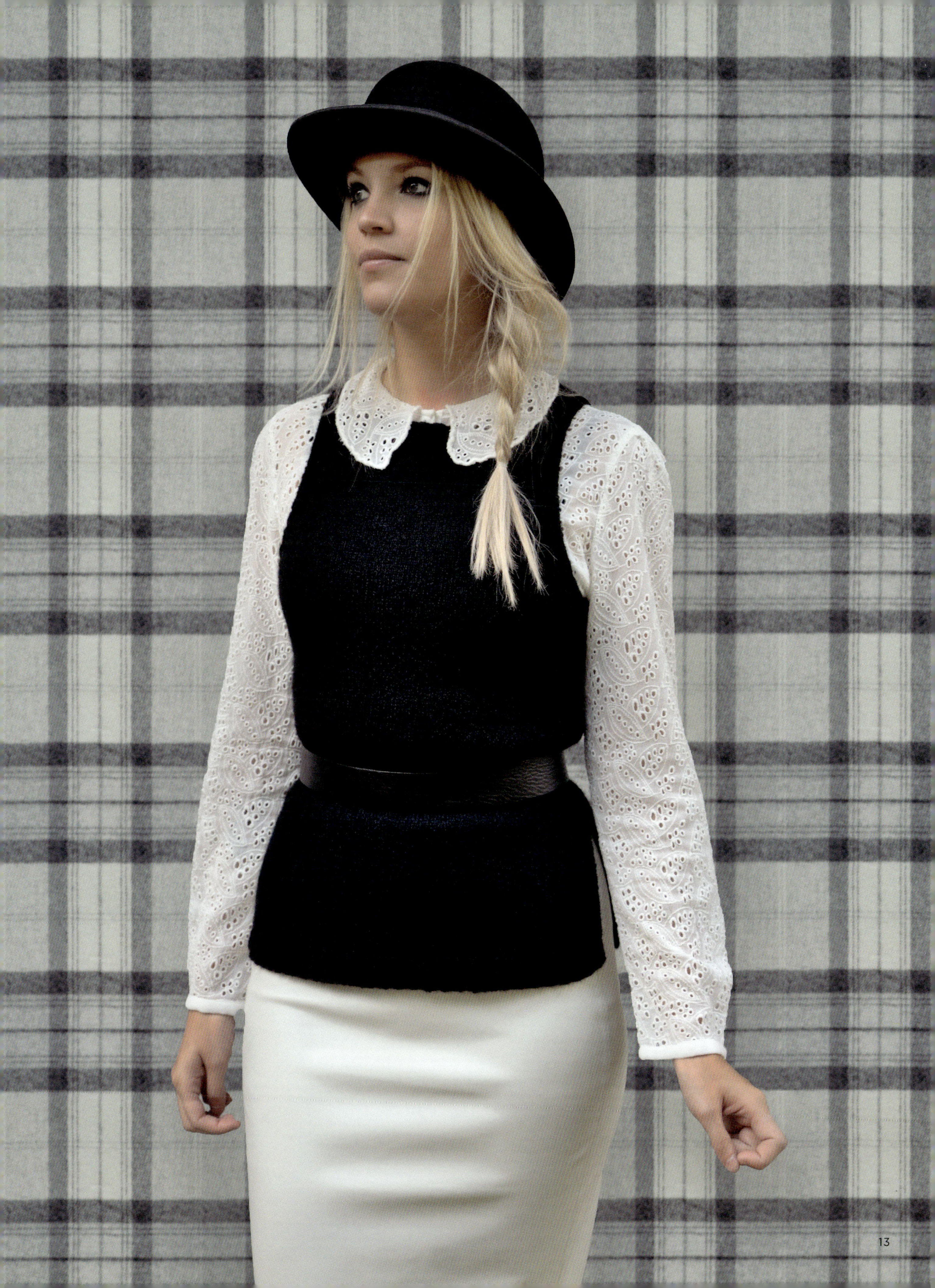

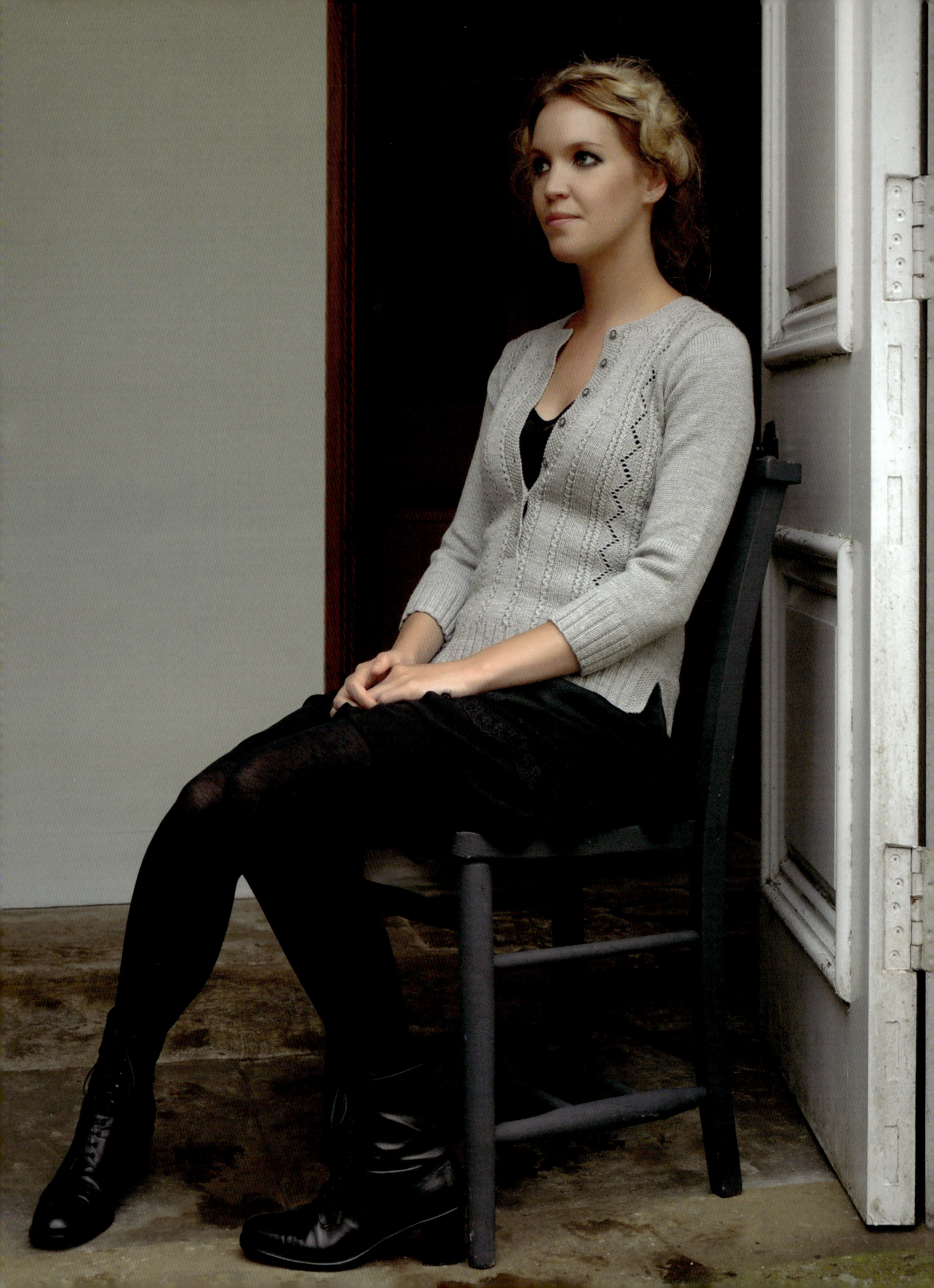

SENTIMENT – a pretty button through sweater with eyelet panels

FEN – a chunky cabled beret

17

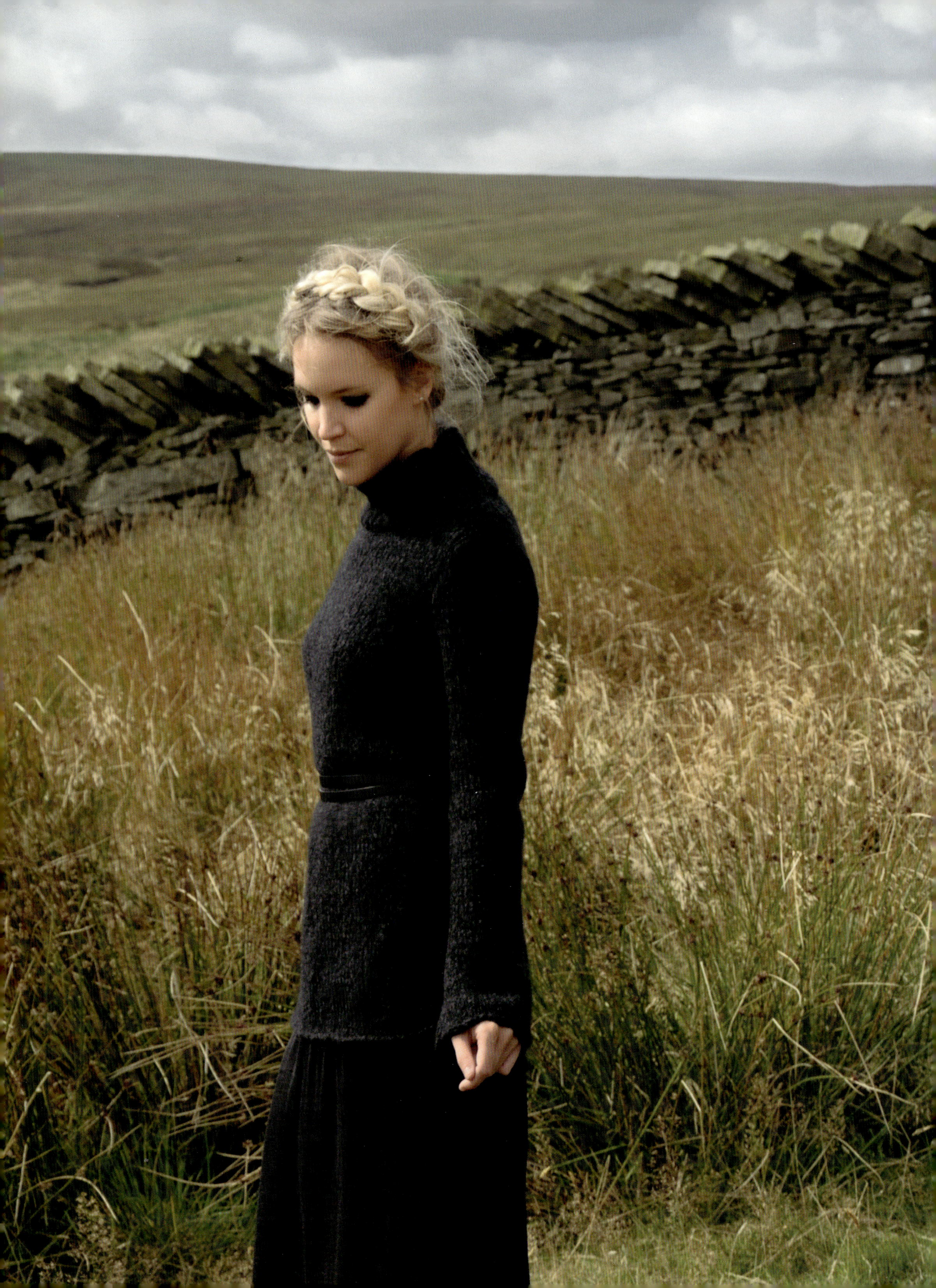

BLACKENED – a longline tunic with deep side vents & flared cuffs.

EMMA – a cropped aran cardigan

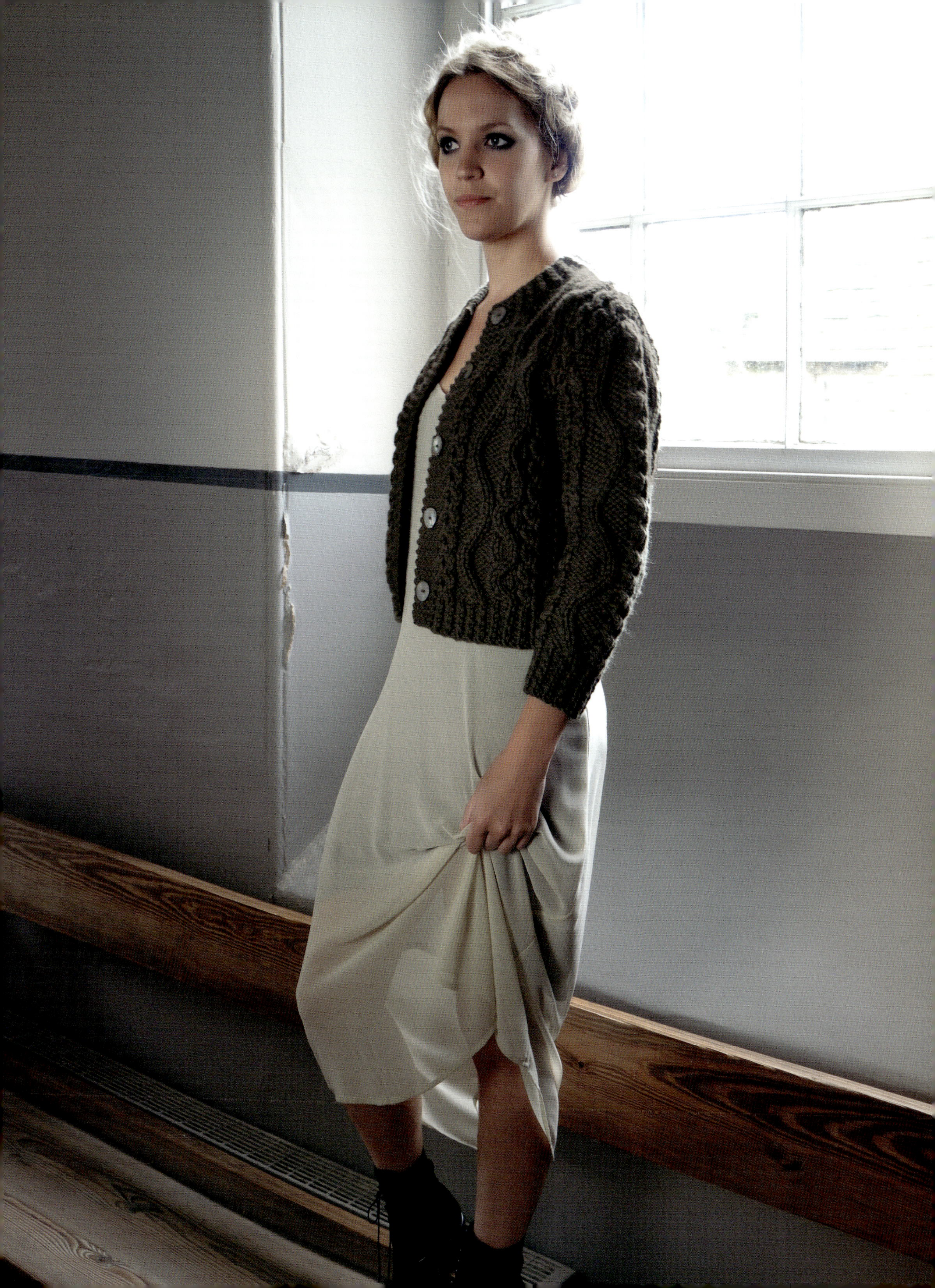

ARGYLE – a patterned cardigan worked in soft natural shades

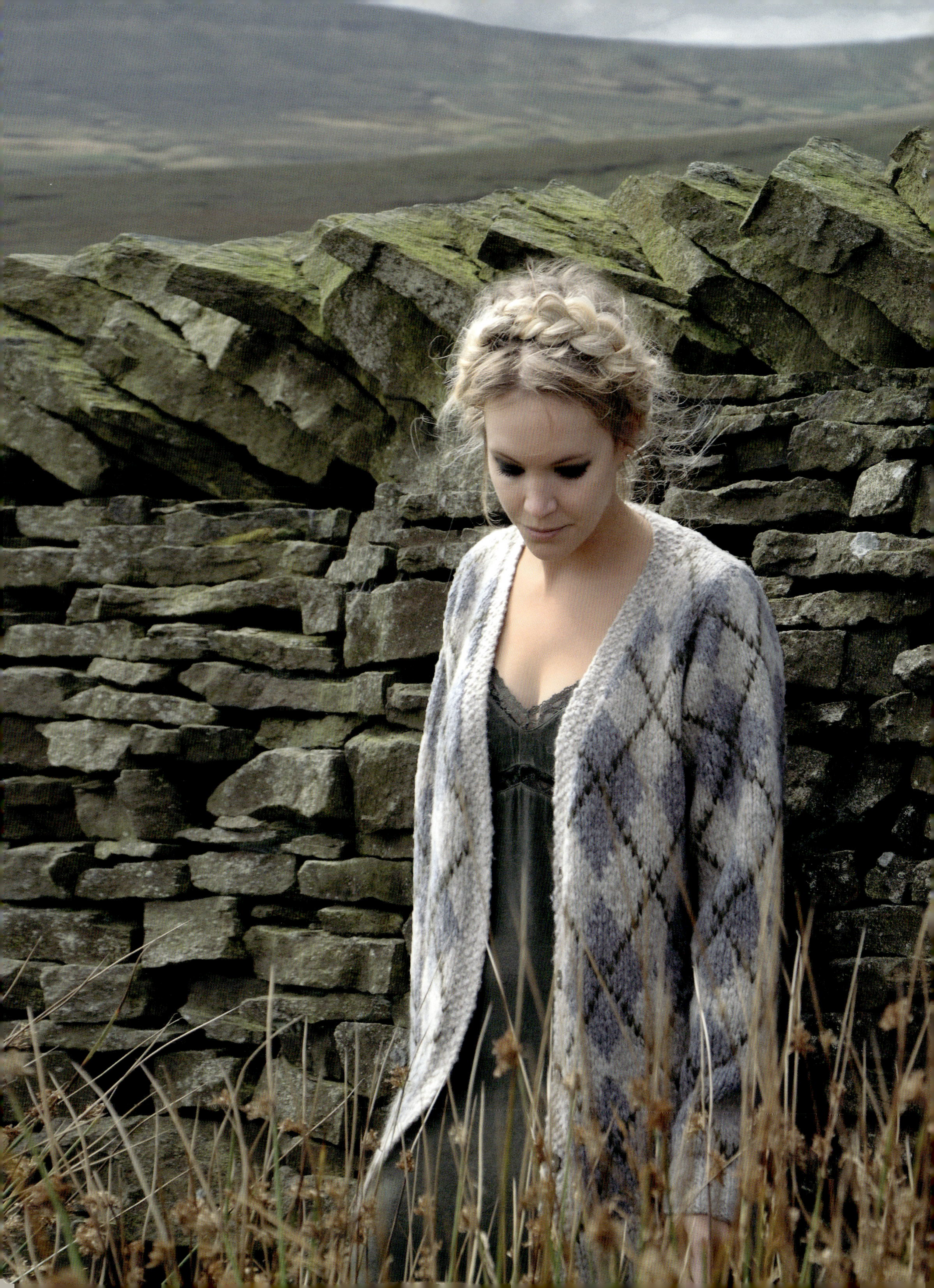

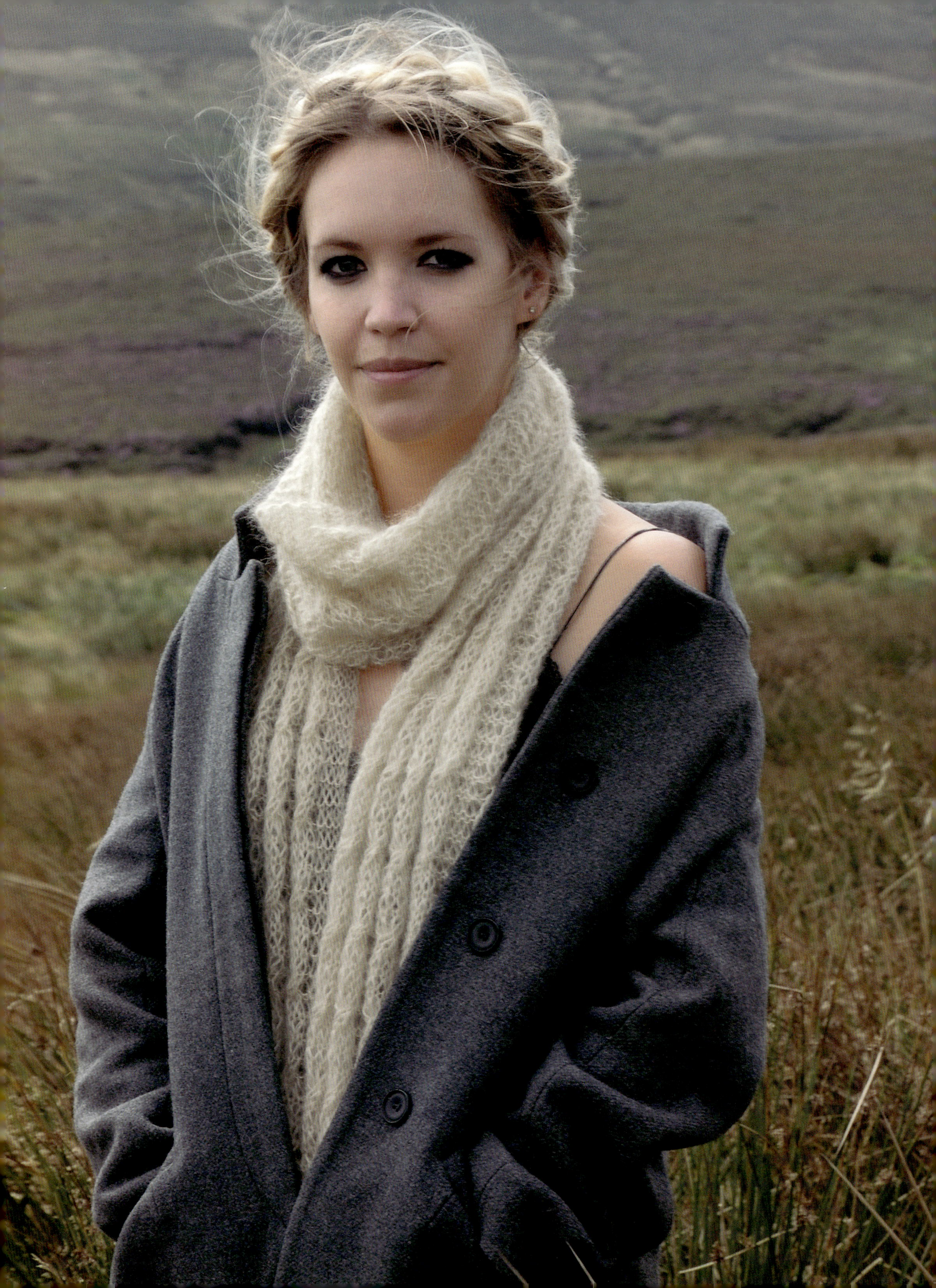

KEEPSAKE – a cosy, softly cabled scarf

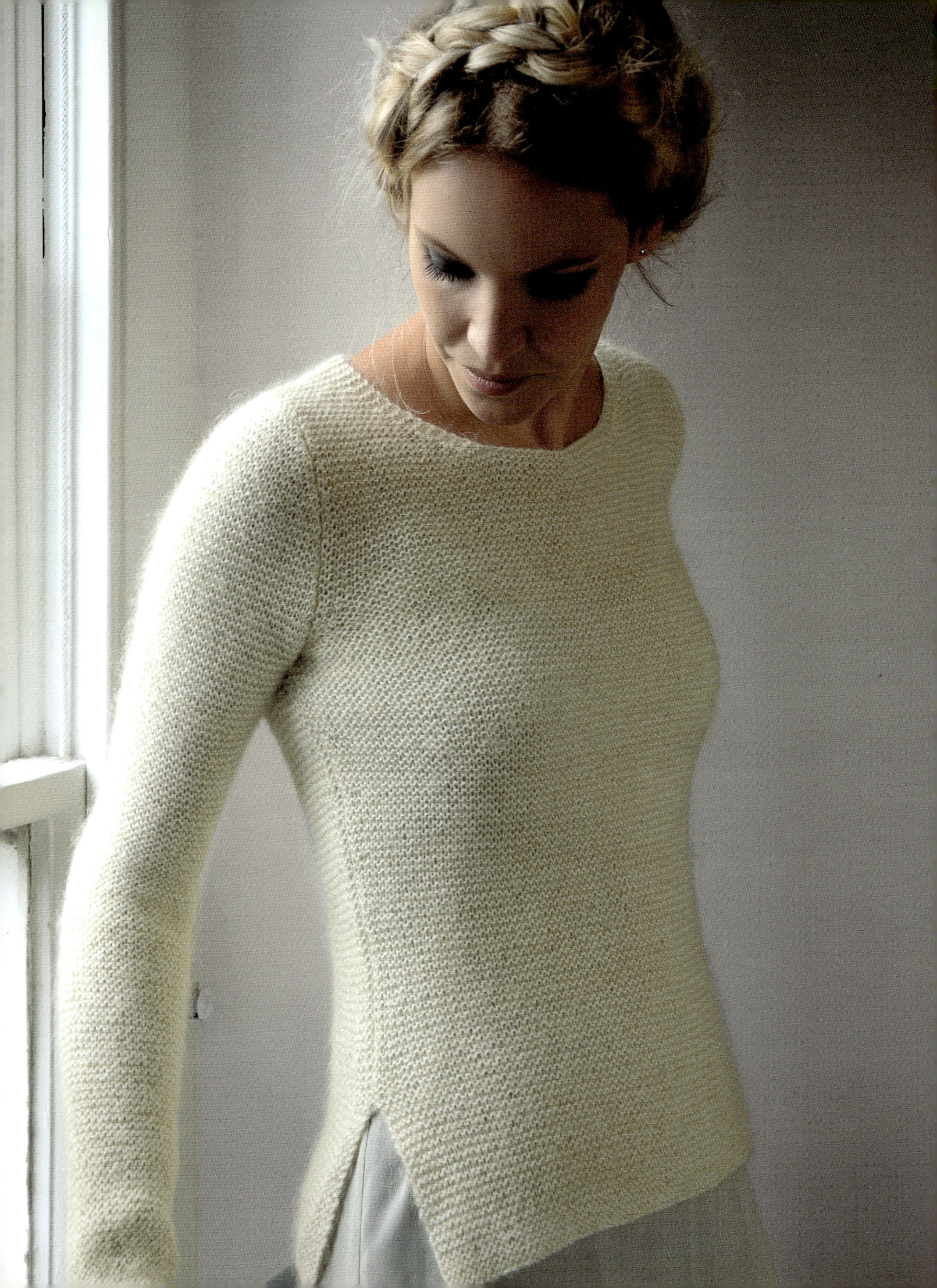

LOVING – a cosy sweater worked in understated garter stitch

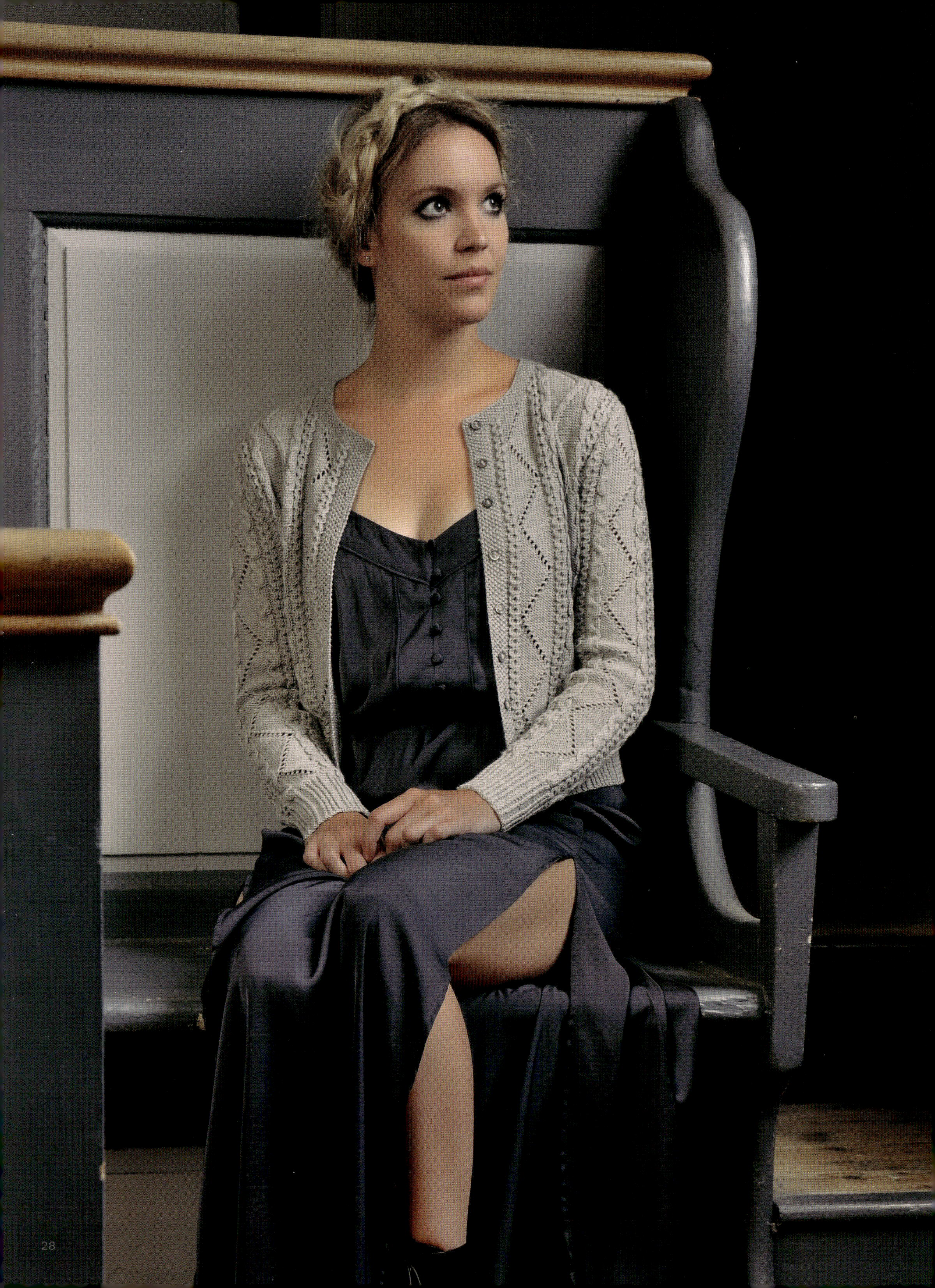

ESCAPE – a neat cardigan worked in eyelet & aran stitches

GIFT – a neat sweater worked in pretty eyelets

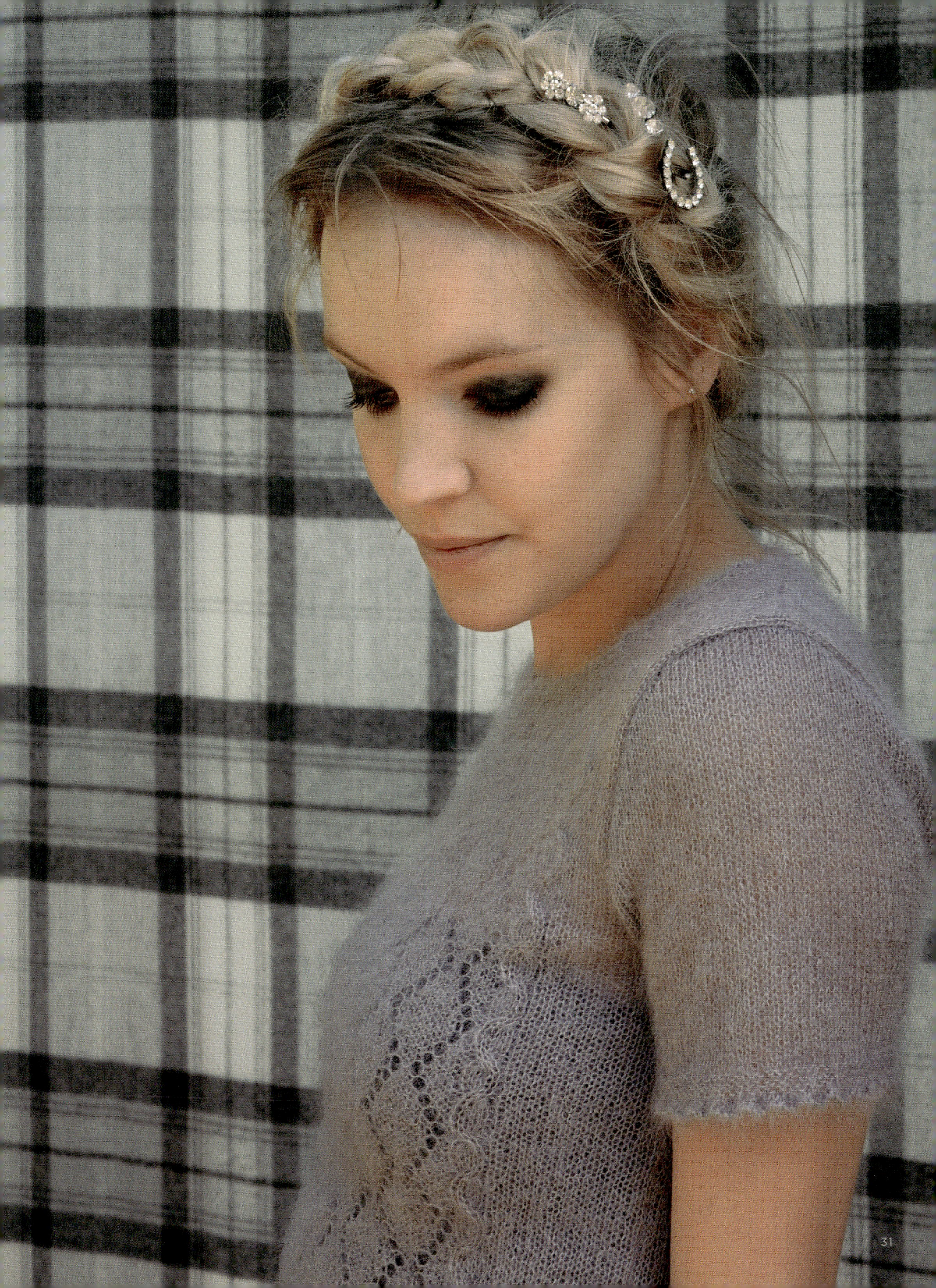

ESME – a feminine take on the classic Boyfriend cardigan

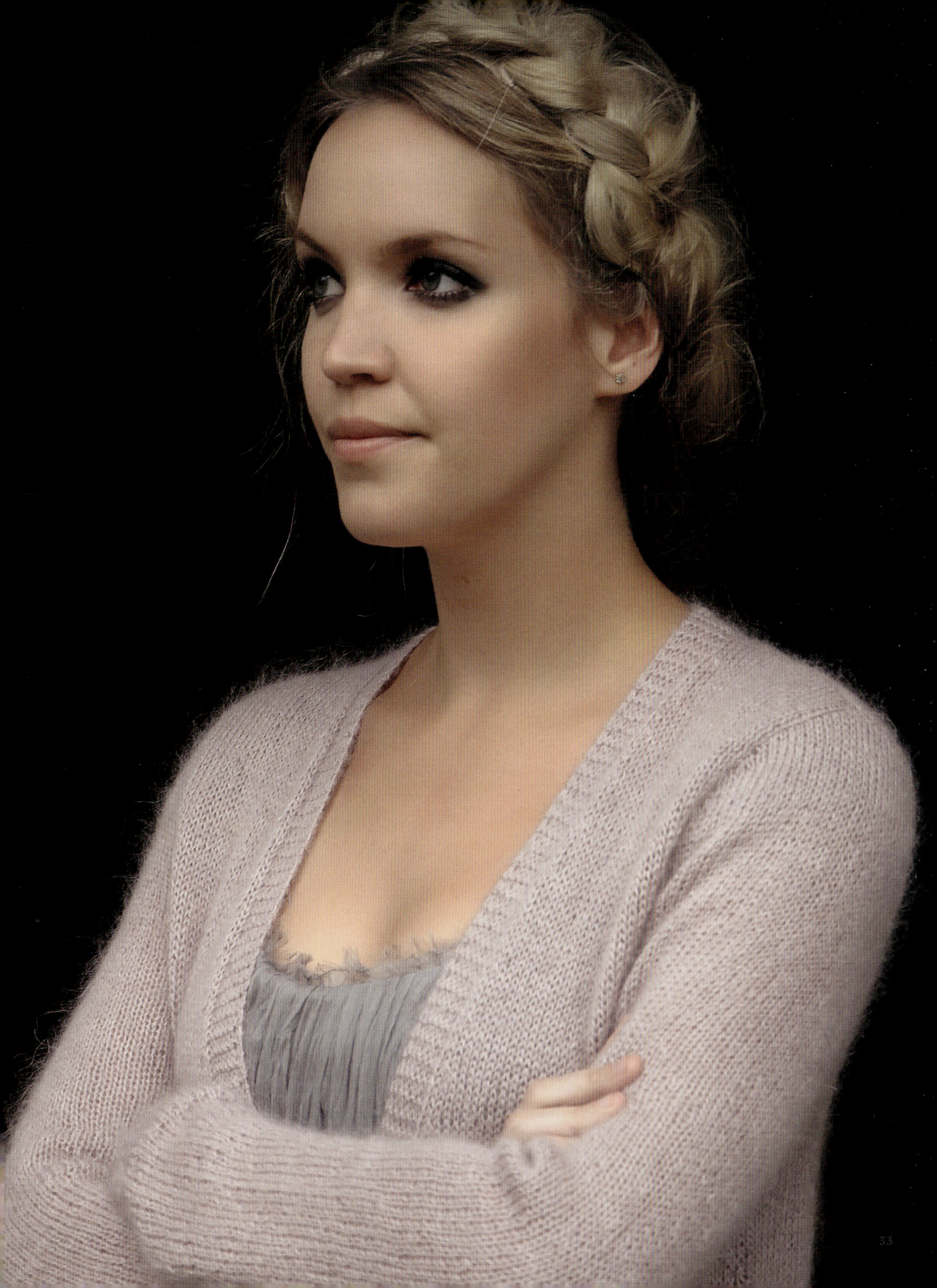

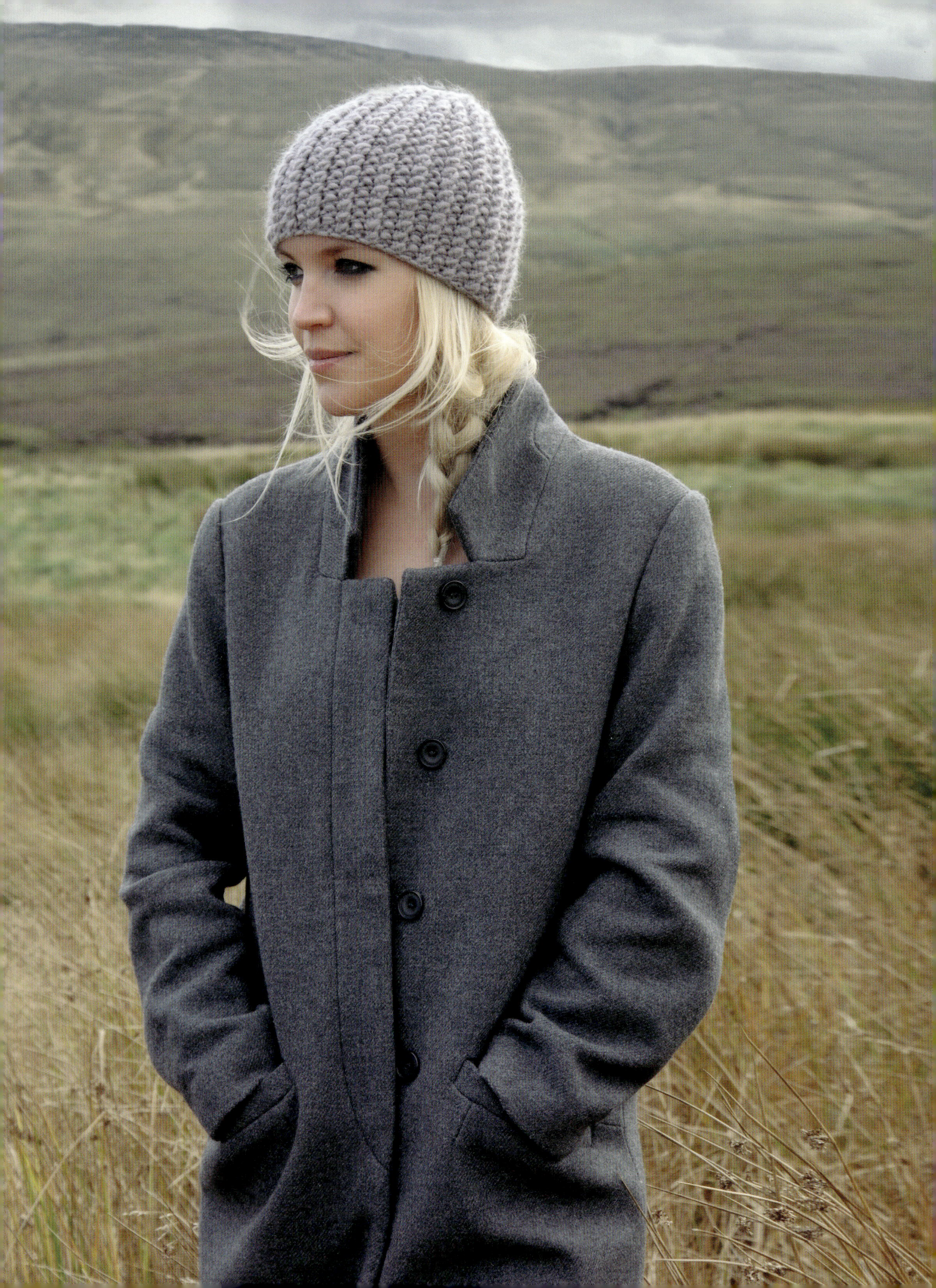

BREE – a neat ribbed hat

SCAPE – a generous
raglan sweater
worked in soft ribbing

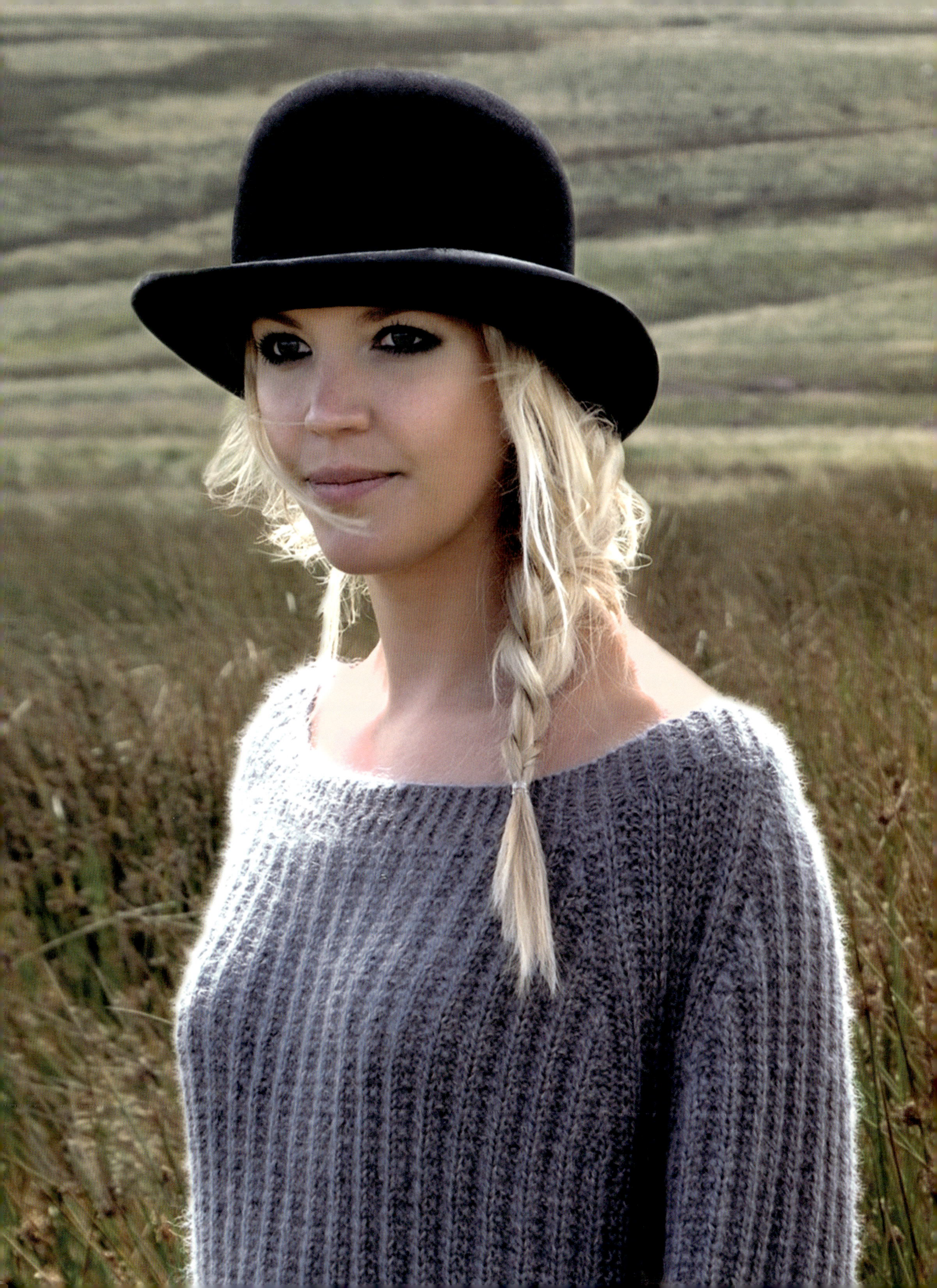

SCAPE — a generous raglan sweater worked in soft ribbing

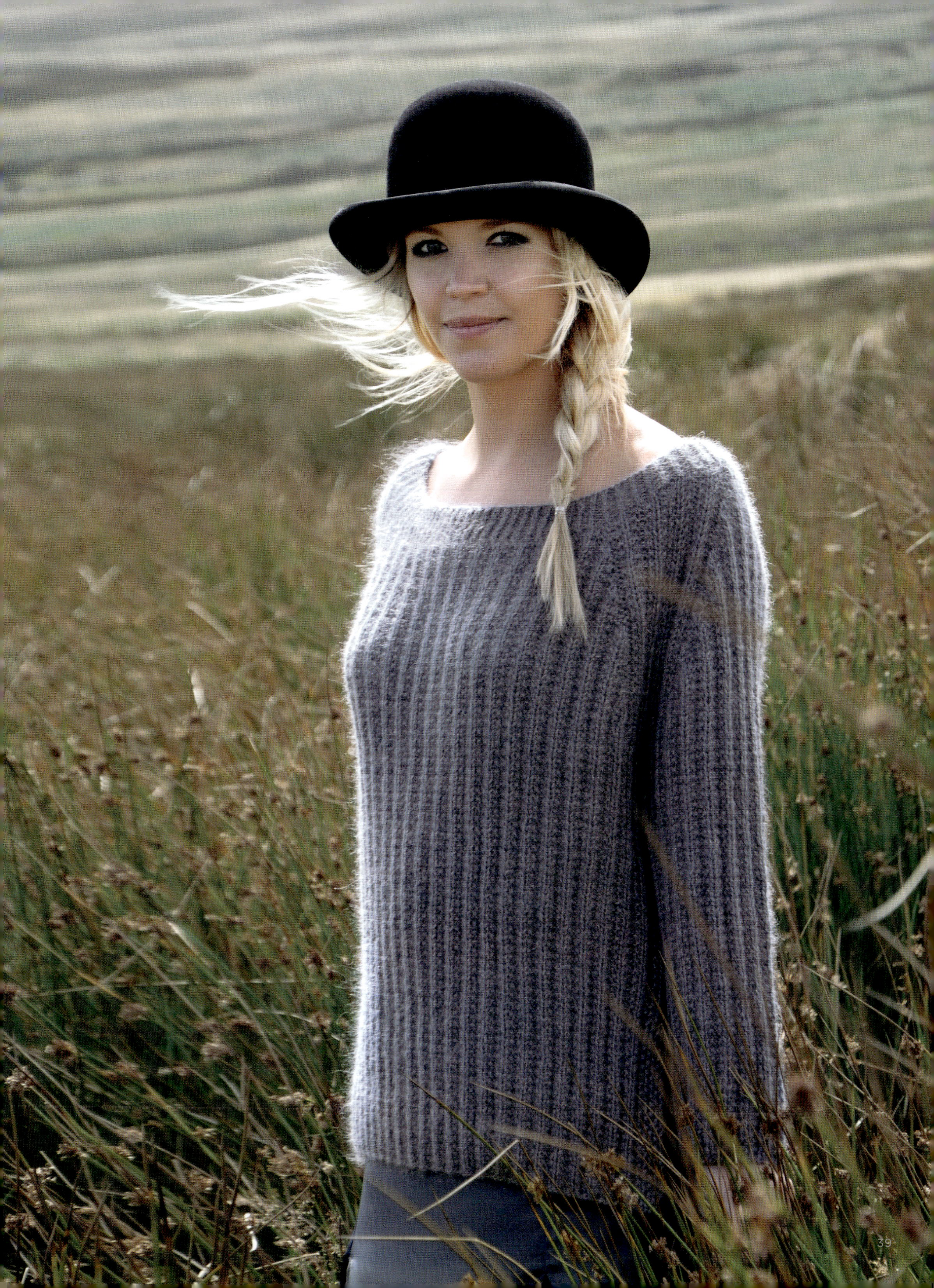

PITCH – a longline sleeveless cardigan with belt & side vents

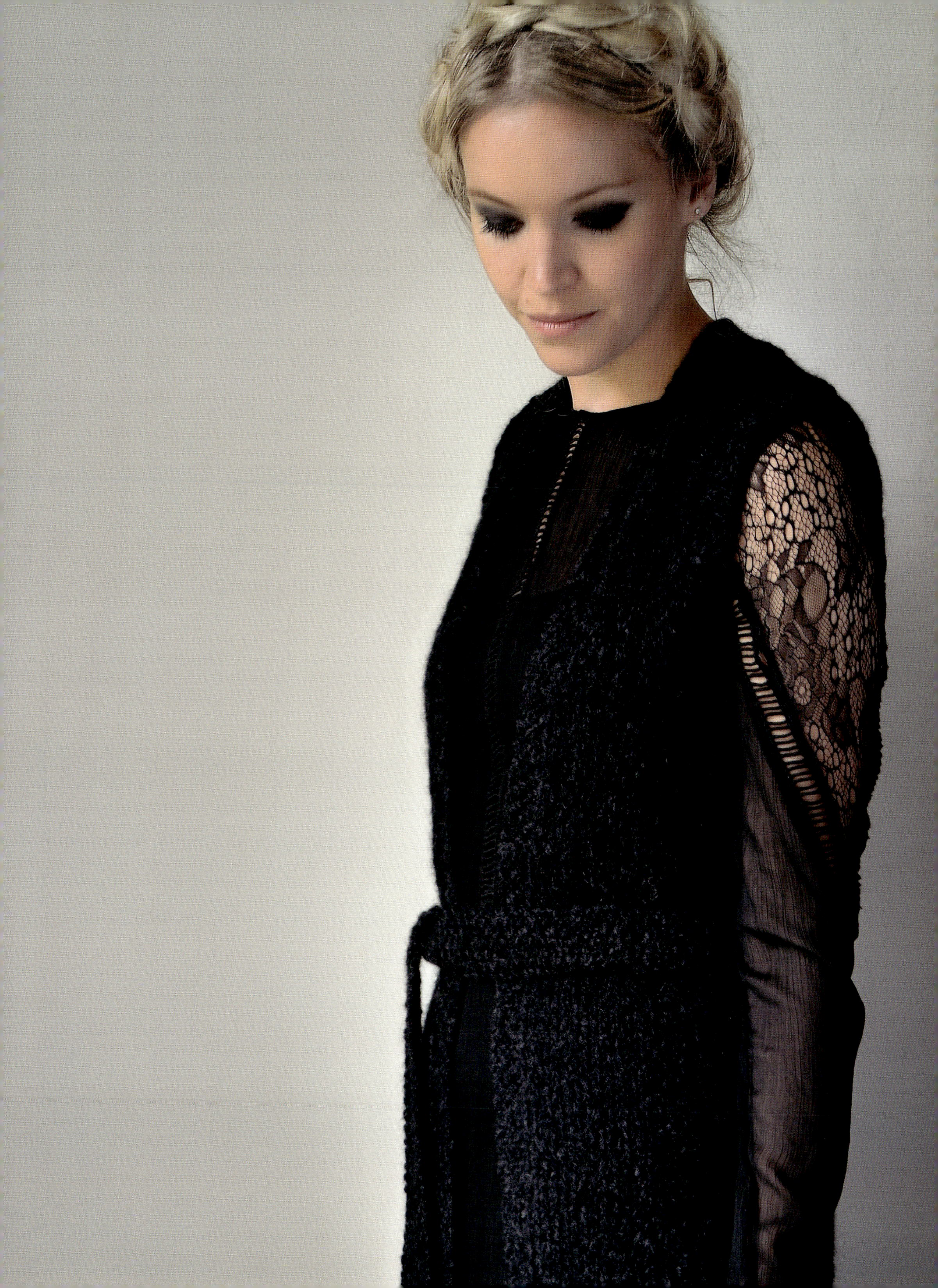

PALE – a pretty garter stitch scarf with eyelet detail

43

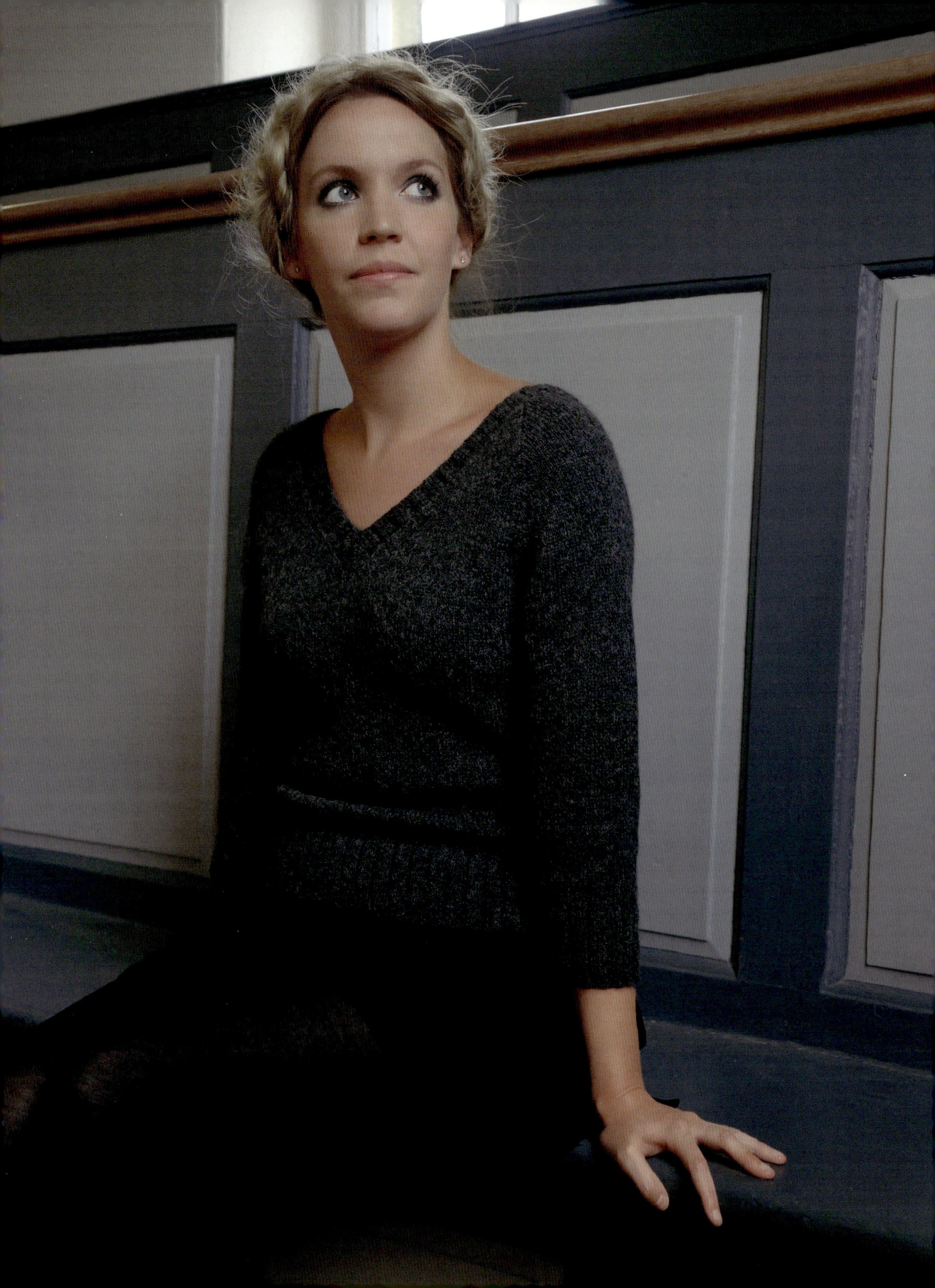

ELIN – a classic sweater with V-neck to both back & front

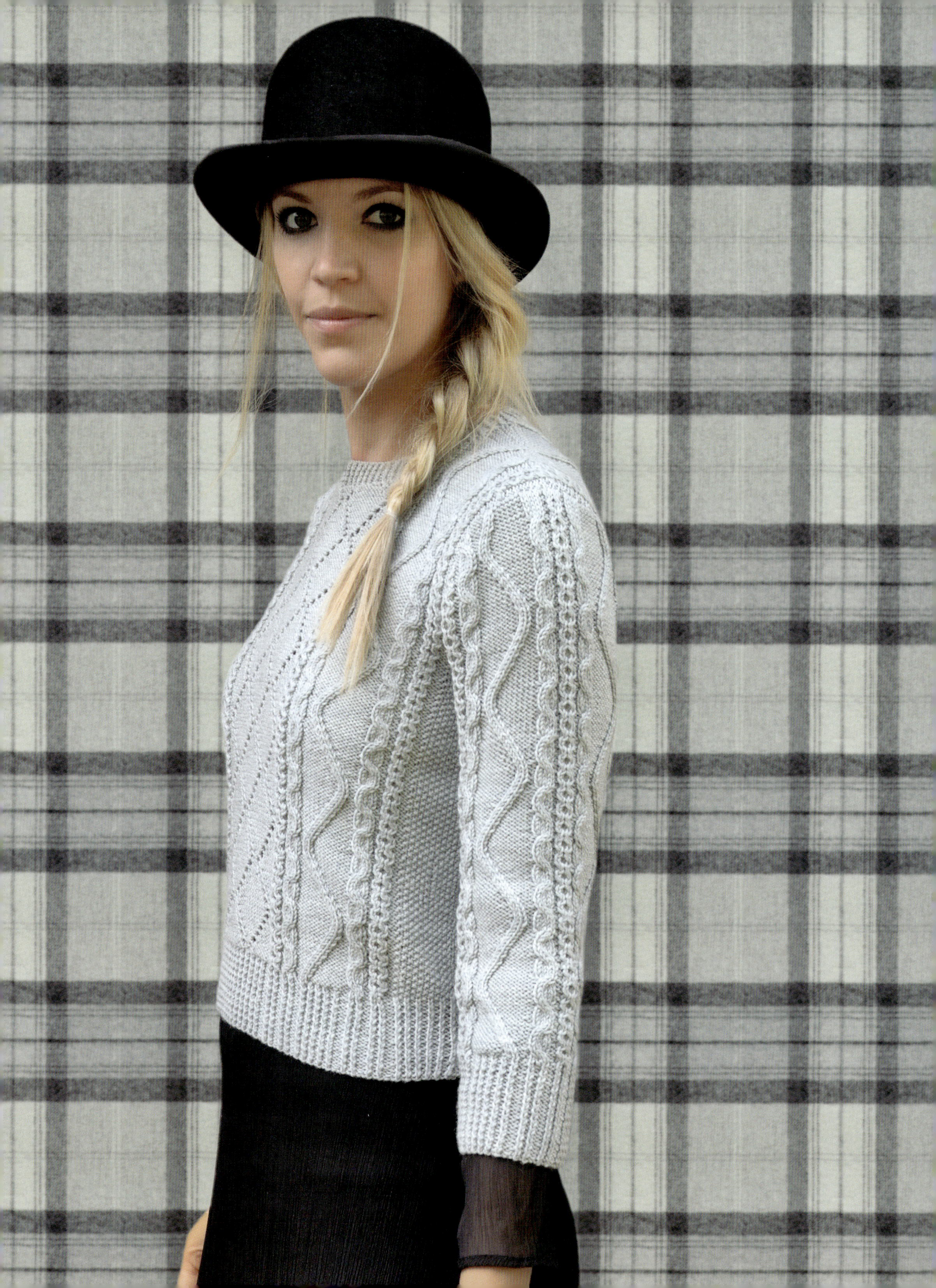

CECILY – a neat sweater worked in eyelet & aran stitches

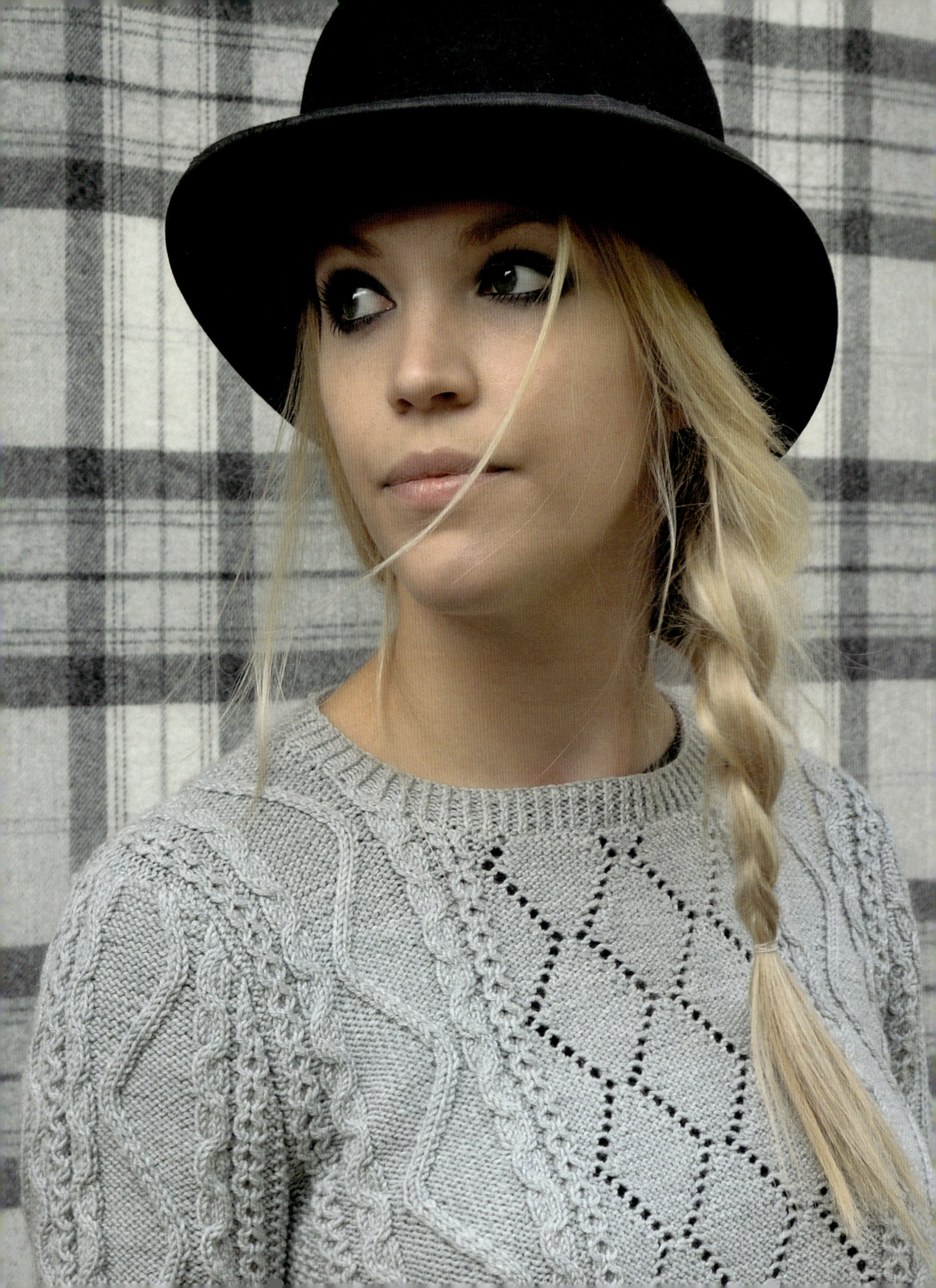

CECILY – a neat sweater worked in eyelet & aran stitches

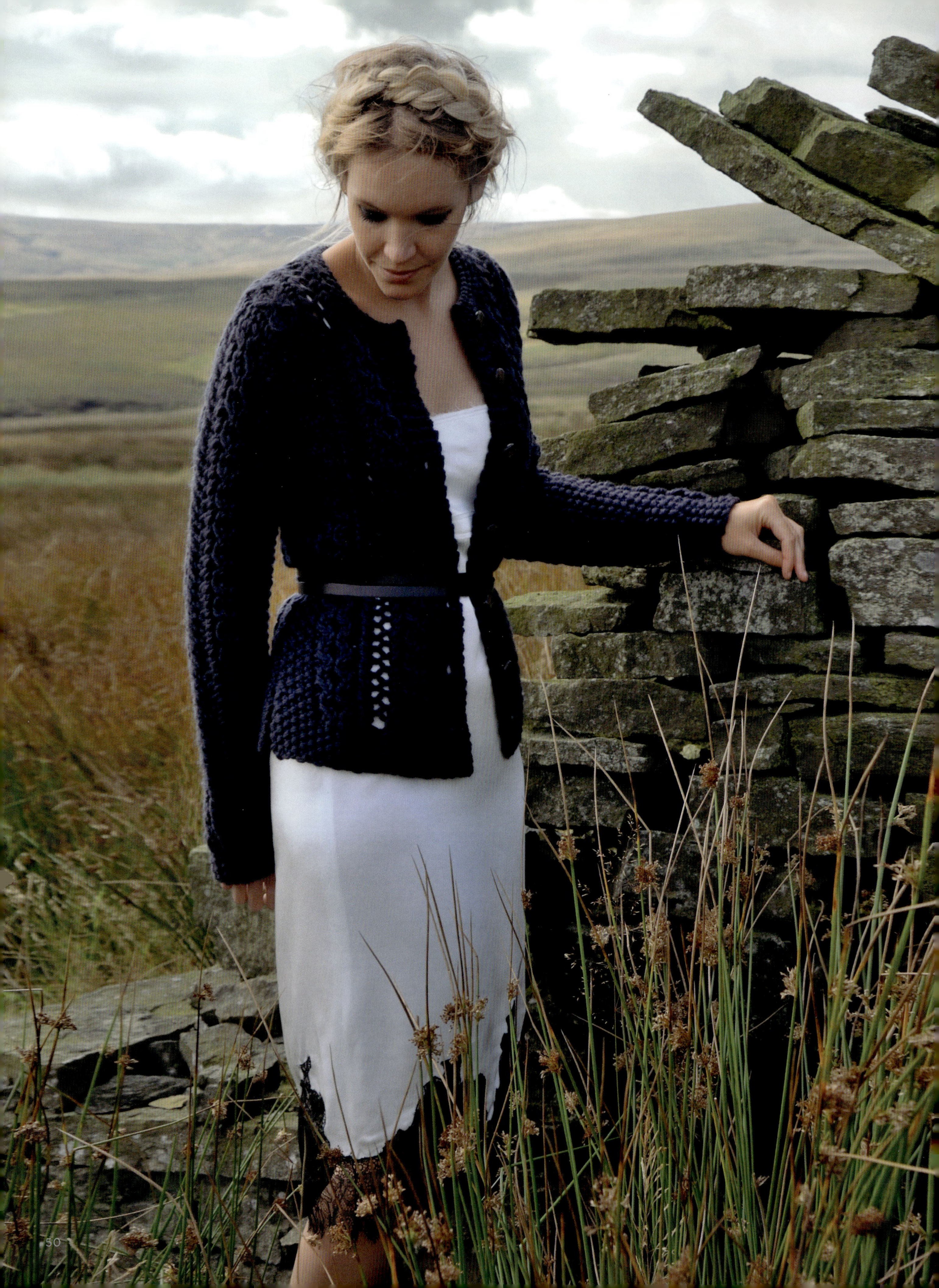

FELL – a fitted cardigan worked in aran braids

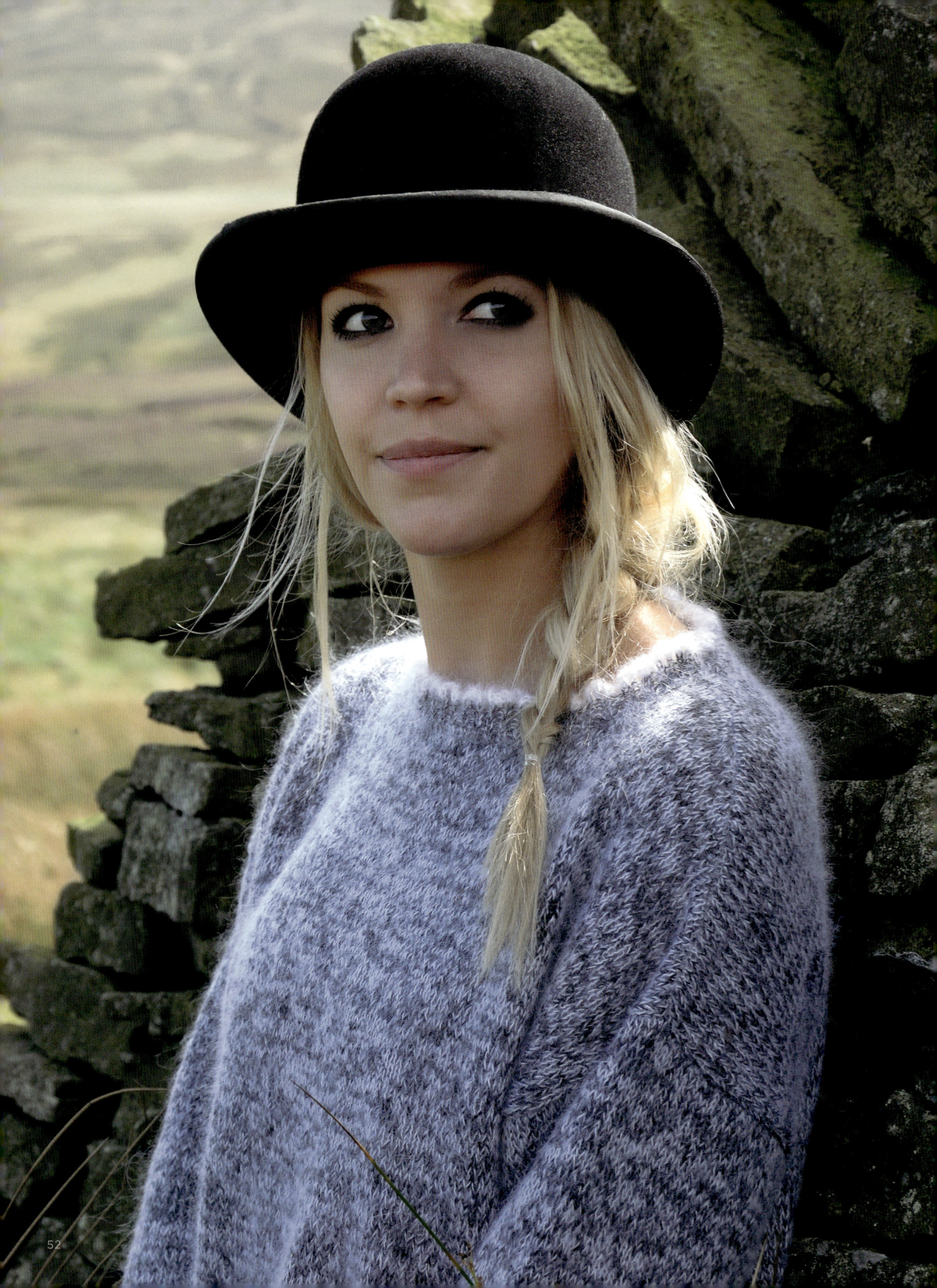

ISLA – a cosy understated sweater with frothy trims

ISLA – a cosy understated sweater with frothy trims

55

JESS
Fitted off the shoulder sweater

Recommendation
Suitable for the knitter with a little experience
Please see pages 10 & 11 for photographs.

	XS	S	M	L	XL	XXL	
To fit bust	81	86	91	97	102	109	cm
	32	34	36	38	40	43	in

Rowan Alpaca Merino DK
12 12 13 13 14 15 x 25gm
Photographed in Walton

Needles
1 pair 2¾mm (no 12) (US 2) needles
1 pair 3¼mm (no 10) (US 3) needles

Tension
27 sts and 39 rows to 10 cm measured over stocking stitch using 3¼mm (US 3) needles.

BACK
Cast on 127 (137: 142: 152: 162: 177) sts using 2¾mm (US 2) needles.
Row 1 (RS): K1, (P1, K1) 3 times, K3, *P2, K3, rep from * to last 7 sts, (K1, P1) 3 times, K1.
Row 2: K1, (P1, K1) 3 times, P3, *K2, P3, rep from * to last 7 sts, (K1, P1) 3 times, K1.
These 2 rows set the sts – 7 sts in moss st at each end of row and rem sts in rib.
Cont as set for a further 17 rows, ending with a **RS** row.
Row 20 (WS): K1, (P1, K1) 3 times, P3, (K2, P3) 1 (0: 1: 1: 0: 0) times, (K2tog, P3) 20 (24: 23: 25: 29: 32) times, (K2, P3) 1 (0: 1: 1: 0: 0) times, (K1, P1) 3 times, K1.
107 (113: 119: 127: 133: 145) sts.
Change to 3¼mm (US 3) needles.
Row 21 (RS): K1, (P1, K1) 3 times, K to last 7 sts, (K1, P1) 3 times, K1.
Row 22: K1, (P1, K1) 3 times, P to last 7 sts, (K1, P1) 3 times, K1.
These 2 rows set the sts – 7 sts still in moss st at each end of row but rem sts now in st st.
Cont as now set for a further 38 rows, ending with a WS row.
Place markers at both ends of last row (to denote top of side seam openings).
Now working **all** sts in st st, cont as follows:
Next row (RS): K10, K2tog tbl, K to last 12 sts, K2tog, K10.
Working all side seam decreases as set by last row, dec 1 st at each end of 4th and 7 foll 4th rows.
89 (95: 101: 109: 115: 127) sts.
Work 17 rows, ending with a WS row.
Next row (RS): K3, M1, K to last 3 sts, M1, K3.
Working all side seam increases as set by last row, inc 1 st at each end of 8th and foll 8th row, then on 6 foll 6th rows.
107 (113: 119: 127: 133: 145) sts.
Cont straight until work measures 44 (44: 45: 45: 45: 45) cm, ending with a WS row.
Shape raglan armholes
Cast off 6 sts at beg of next 2 rows.
95 (101: 107: 115: 121: 133) sts.
Next row (RS): K2, K2tog, K to last 4 sts, K2tog tbl, K2.
Working all raglan armhole decreases as set by last row, cont as follows:
Dec 1 st at each end of 4th (2nd: 2nd: 2nd: 2nd: 2nd) and foll 0 (1: 7: 11: 15: 25) alt rows, then on 10 (11: 8: 7: 6: 2) foll 4th rows.
71 (73: 73: 75: 75: 75) sts.
Work 1 row, ending with a WS row.
Cast off.

FRONT
Work as given for back until 81 (83: 83: 87: 87: 93) sts rem in raglan armhole shaping.
Work 3 (3: 3: 3: 3: 1) rows, ending with RS facing for next row.
Shape front neck
Next row (RS): K2, K2tog, K10 (10: 10: 12: 12: 15) and turn, leaving rem sts on a holder.
13 (13: 13: 15: 15: 18) sts.
Work each side of neck separately.
Keeping raglan armhole decreases correct as set, dec 1 st at raglan armhole edge of 4th (4th: 4th: 4th: 4th: 2nd) and foll 0 (0: 0: 0: 0: 5) alt rows, then on 2 (2: 2: 3: 3: 1) foll 4th rows **and at same time** dec 1 st at neck edge of next 6 rows, then on foll 2 alt rows, then on 0 (0: 0: 1: 1: 1) foll 4th row.
2 sts.
Work 1 row, ending with a WS row.
Next row (RS): K2tog and fasten off.
With RS facing, rejoin yarn to rem sts, cast off centre 53 (55: 55: 55: 55: 55) sts, K to last 4 sts, K2tog tbl, K2.
13 (13: 13: 15: 15: 18) sts.
Complete to match first side, reversing shapings.

SLEEVES (both alike)
Cast on 55 (57: 59: 63: 65: 67) sts using 2¾mm (US 2) needles.
Row 1 (RS): P1 (2: 0: 0: 1: 2), K3 (3: 1: 3: 3: 3), *P2, K3, rep from * to last 1 (2: 3: 0: 1: 2) sts, P1 (2: 2: 0: 1: 2), K0 (0: 1: 0: 0: 0).
Row 2: K1 (2: 0: 0: 1: 2), P3 (3: 1: 3: 3: 3), *K2, P3, rep from * to last 1 (2: 3: 0: 1: 2) sts, K1 (2: 2: 0: 1: 2), P0 (0: 1: 0: 0: 0).
These 2 rows form rib.
Work in rib for a further 22 rows, ending with a WS row.
Change to 3¼mm (US 3) needles.
Beg with a K row, now work in st st throughout as follows:

Working all sleeve increases in same way as side seam increases, inc 1 st at each end of 3rd and every foll 10th (12th: 12th: 14th: 12th: 12th) row to 59 (79: 63: 83: 75: 87) sts, then on every foll 12th (14th: 14th: 16th: 14th: 14th) row until there are 79 (81: 81: 85: 89: 93) sts.
Cont straight until sleeve measures 45 (46: 47: 48: 49: 50) cm, ending with a WS row.

Shape raglan
Cast off 6 sts at beg of next 2 rows.
67 (69: 69: 73: 77: 81) sts.
Work 4 (4: 4: 0: 0: 0) rows.
Working all raglan decreases in same way as raglan armhole decreases, dec 1 st at each end of next and foll 0 (0: 0: 0: 2: 4) alt rows, then on foll 4th row until 47 sts rem.
Work 1 row, ending with a WS row.

Left sleeve only
Work 1 row.
Cast off 16 sts at beg of next row, dec 1 st at beg (raglan edge) of foll row, then cast off 15 sts at beg of next row.

Right sleeve only
Cast off 16 sts at beg of next row.
Work 1 row.
Cast off 15 sts at beg and dec 1 st at end (raglan edge) of next row.
Work 1 row.

Both sleeves
Cast off rem 15 sts.

MAKING UP
Press all pieces with a warm iron over a damp cloth.
Join both front and right back raglan seams using back stitch or mattress stitch if preferred.

Neckband
With RS facing and using 2¾mm (US 2) needles, pick up and knit 44 sts from top of left sleeve, 12 (12: 12: 14: 14: 14) sts down left side of front neck, 54 sts from front, 12 (12: 12: 14: 14: 14) sts up right side of front neck, 44 sts from top of right sleeve, then 68 (72: 72: 72: 72: 72) sts from back.
234 (238: 238: 242: 242: 242) sts.
Row 1 (WS): K2, *P2, K2, rep from * to end.
Row 2: P2, *K1, yfwd, K1, P2, rep from * to end.
292 (297: 297: 302: 302: 302) sts.
Row 3: K2, *P3, K2, rep from * to end.
Row 4: P2, *K3, P2, rep from * to end.
Last 2 rows form rib.
Cont in rib for a further 7 rows, ending with a WS row.

Row 12 (RS): P2, (K3, P2tog) 10 times, rib 103 (103: 103: 108: 108: 108), (P2tog, K3) 10 times, rib 87 (92: 92: 92: 92: 92).
272 (277: 277: 282: 282: 282) sts.
Cast off in rib (on **WS**).
Join left back raglan and neckband seam.
Join side and sleeve seams, leaving side seams open below markers.

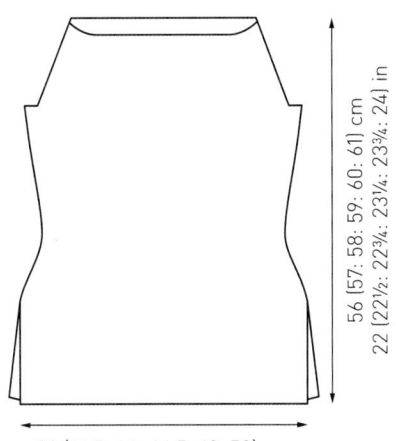

39 (41.5: 44: 46.5: 49: 53) cm
15½ (16½: 17½: 18½: 19½: 21) in

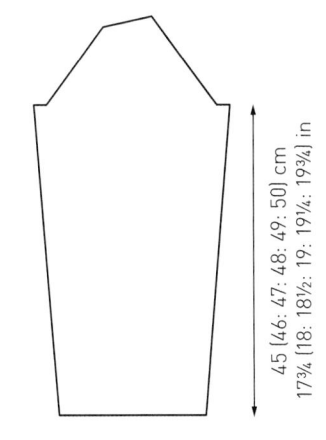

56 (57: 58: 59: 60: 61) cm
22 (22½: 22¾: 23¼: 23¾: 24) in

45 (46: 47: 48: 49: 50) cm
17¾ (18: 18½: 19: 19¼: 19¾) in

BARRETT
Simply striped sweater

Recommendation
Suitable for the knitter with a little experience
Please see pages 7, 8 & 9 for photographs.

	XS	S	M	L	XL	XXL	
To fit bust	81	86	91	97	102	109	cm
	32	34	36	38	40	43	in

Rowan Kidsilk Haze

| A White | 3 | 3 | 3 | 4 | 4 | 5 | x 25gm |
| B Wicked | 3 | 3 | 3 | 4 | 4 | 5 | x 25gm |

Needles
1 pair 4mm (no 8) (US 6) needles
1 pair 4½mm (no 7) (US 7) needles
1 pair 8mm (no 0) (US 11) needles
1 pair 9mm (no 00) (US 13) needles

Tension
12 sts and 19 rows to 10 cm measured over pattern using a combination of 4½mm (US 7) and 9mm (US 13) needles and yarn DOUBLE.

BACK
Cast on 56 (58: 62: 64: 68: 72) sts using 8mm (US 11) needles and yarn A DOUBLE.
Row 1 (RS): Using a 4mm (US 6) needle, knit.
Row 2: Using a 8mm (US 11) needle, purl.
Rep last 2 rows once more.
Join in yarn B DOUBLE.
Using yarn B DOUBLE, rep rows 1 and 2 twice more, ending with a WS row.
Now work in patt as follows:
Row 1 (RS): Using a 4½mm (US 7) needle and yarn A DOUBLE, knit.
Row 2: Using a 9mm (US 13) needle and yarn A DOUBLE, purl.
Rows 3 and 4: As rows 1 and 2.
Row 5: Using a 4½mm (US 7) needle and yarn B DOUBLE, knit.
Row 6: Using a 9mm (US 13) needle and yarn B DOUBLE, purl.
Rows 7 and 8: As rows 5 and 6.
Last 8 rows form patt.**
Cont in patt until back measures approx 40 (40: 41: 41: 41: 41) cm, ending after 4 (4: 2: 2: 2: 2) rows using yarn A (A: B: B: B: B) and with a WS row.
Shape armholes
Keeping patt and stripes correct, cast off 3 (3: 4: 4: 5: 5) sts at beg of next 2 rows.
50 (52: 54: 56: 58: 62) sts.
Dec 1 st at each end of next 1 (1: 1: 3: 3: 3) rows, then on foll 2 (2: 2: 1: 1: 2) alt rows, then on foll 4th row.
42 (44: 46: 46: 48: 50) sts.
Cont straight until armhole measures 17 (18: 18: 19: 20: 21) cm, ending with a **RS** row.
Shape back neck and shoulders
Keeping patt and stripes correct, cont as follows:
Next row (WS): P13 (13: 14: 13: 14: 15) and slip these sts onto a holder, cast off next 16 (18: 18: 20: 20: 20) sts **knitwise**, P to end.
13 (13: 14: 13: 14: 15) sts.
Work each side of neck separately.
Next row (RS): Cast off 4 sts, K to last 4 sts, K2tog tbl, K2. 8 (8: 9: 8: 9: 10) sts.
Next row: P2, P2tog tbl, P to end.
Cast off 4 sts at beg of next row.
Work 1 row.
Cast off rem 3 (3: 4: 3: 4: 5) sts.
With RS facing, rejoin appropriate yarn to sts on holder and K2, K2tog, K to end.
Complete to match first side, reversing shapings.

FRONT
Work as given for back until 17 (17: 17: 19: 19: 19) rows less have been worked than on back to start of shoulder shaping, ending with a **RS** row.
Shape front neck
Keeping patt and stripes correct, cont as follows:
Next row (WS): P17 (17: 18: 18: 19: 20) and slip these sts onto a holder, cast off next 8 (10: 10: 10: 10: 10) sts **knitwise**, P to end.
17 (17: 18: 18: 19: 20) sts.
Work each side of neck separately.
Next row (RS): K to last 4 sts, K2tog tbl, K2.
Working all neck decreases as set by last row, dec 1 st at neck edge of 2nd and foll 3 (3: 3: 4: 4: 4) alt rows, then on foll 4th row.
11 (11: 12: 11: 12: 13) sts.
Work 3 rows, ending with a WS row.
Shape shoulder
Cast off 4 sts at beg of next and foll alt row.
Work 1 row.
Cast off rem 3 (3: 4: 3: 4: 5) sts.
With RS facing, rejoin appropriate yarn to sts on holder and K2, K2tog, K to end.
Complete to match first side, reversing shapings.

SLEEVES (both alike)
Cast on 24 (26: 28: 28: 30: 30) sts using 8mm (US 11) needles and yarn A DOUBLE.
Work as given for back from ** to **.
Cont in patt, shaping sides by inc 1 st at each end of 5th and every foll 12th (12th: 14th: 10th: 10th: 10th) row to 30 (32: 40: 32: 34: 46) sts, then on every foll 14th (14th: -: 12th: 12th: -) row until there are 36 (38: -: 42: 44: -) sts.
Cont straight until sleeve measures approx 52 (52: 53: 53: 53: 53) cm, ending after 4 (4: 2: 2: 2: 2) rows using yarn A (A: B: B: B: B) and with a WS row.

Continued on next page...

BREE
Neat ribbed hat

Recommendation
Suitable for the knitter with a little experience
Please see pages 34 & 35 for photographs.

Rowan Cocoon
1 x 100gm
Photographed in Dove

Needles
1 pair 7mm (no 2) (US 10½) needles
1 pair 8mm (no 0) (US 11) needles

Tension
11 sts and 20 rows to 10 cm measured over pattern using 8mm (US 11) needles.

HAT
Cast on 49 sts using 7mm (US 10½) needles.
Row 1 (RS): K1, *inc in next st (by working into front and back of st), rep from * to last st, K1.
Row 2: K1, P2tog, *K2tog, P2tog, rep from * to last st, K1.
These 2 rows form patt. (**Note**: As the number of sts increases when working patt row 1, count sts after patt row 2 **only**.)
Work in patt for a further 6 rows, ending with a WS row.
Change to 8mm (US 11) needles.
Cont in patt until hat measures 17 cm, ending with a WS row.
Shape top
Row 1 (RS): K1, *inc once in each of next 5 sts, K3tog leaving these 3 sts on left needle, then K the same 3 sts tog but tbl – 2 sts decreased but 2 sts on right needle (extra st is decreased on next row), rep from * to end.
Work 3 rows. 37 sts.

Row 5: K1, *inc once in each of next 3 sts, K3tog leaving these 3 sts on left needle, then K the same 3 sts tog but tbl – 2 sts decreased but 2 sts on right needle (extra st is decreased on next row), rep from * to end.
Work 1 row. 25 sts.
Row 7: K1, *K1, P3tog, rep from * to end.
13 sts.
Break yarn and thread through rem 13 sts.
Pull up tight and fasten off securely.
Sew back seam.

BARRET – *Continued from previous page.*

Shape top
Keeping patt and stripes correct, cast off 3 (3: 4: 4: 5: 5) sts at beg of next 2 rows.
30 (32: 32: 34: 34: 36) sts.
Dec 1 st at each end of next and 3 foll 4th rows, then on every foll alt row until 18 sts rem, then on foll 3 rows, ending with a WS row.
Cast off rem 12 sts.

MAKING UP
Press all pieces with a warm iron over a damp cloth.
Join both shoulder seams using back stitch or mattress stitch if preferred.
Join side seams. Join sleeve seams.
Insert sleeves into armholes.

45.5 (48: 50.5: 53: 55.5: 59.5) cm
18 (19: 20: 21: 22: 22½) in

57 [58: 59: 60: 61: 62] cm
22½ [22¾: 23¼: 23¾: 24: 24½] in

52 [52: 53: 53: 53: 53] cm
20½ [20½: 21: 21: 21: 21] in

CECILY
Neat sweater worked in eyelet & aran stitches

Recommendation
Suitable for the more experienced knitter
Please see pages 46, 47 & 48 for photographs.

	XS	S	M	L	XL	XXL	
To fit bust	81	86	91	97	102	109	cm
	32	34	36	38	40	43	in

Rowan Super Fine Merino 4 ply
7 8 8 9 9 10 x 50gm
Photographed in Marble

Needles
1 pair 2¾mm (no 12) (US 2) needles
1 pair 3¼mm (no 10) (US 3) needles
Cable needle

Tension
Based on a stocking stitch tension of 27 sts and 38 rows to 10 cm using 3¼mm (US 3) needles.

Special abbreviations
C4B = slip next 2 sts onto cn and leave at back of work, K2, then K2 from cn; **C4F** = slip next 2 sts onto cn and leave at front of work, K2, then K2 from cn; **cn** = cable needle; **Cr3L** = slip next 2 sts onto cn and leave at front of work, P1, then K2 from cn; **Cr3R** = slip next st onto cn and leave at back of work, K2, then P1 from cn; **Tw2L** = K into back of second st on left needle, then K first st and slip both sts off left needle together; **Tw2R** = K into front of second st on left needle, then K first st and slip both sts off left needle together.

BACK
Cast on 113 (119: 125: 133: 139: 151) sts using 2¾mm (US 2) needles.
Row 1 (RS): P1 (0: 1: 1: 0: 0), (P1, K1 tbl) 4 (6: 7: 9: 11: 14) times, (P2, K1 tbl, P1, K1 tbl) 3 times, (P1, K1 tbl) twice, (P1, K1 tbl, P2, K1 tbl) 3 times, (P1, K1 tbl) 13 times, P1, (K1 tbl, P2, K1 tbl, P1) 3 times, (K1 tbl, P1) twice, (K1 tbl, P1, K1 tbl, P2) 3 times, (K1 tbl, P1) 4 (6: 7: 9: 11: 14) times, P1 (0: 1: 1: 0: 0).
Row 2: K1 (0: 1: 1: 0: 0), (K1, P1) 4 (6: 7: 9: 11: 14) times, (K2, P1, K1, P1) 3 times, (K1, P1) twice, (K1, P1, K2, P1) 3 times, (K1, P1) 13 times, K1, (P1, K2, P1, K1) 3 times, (P1, K1) twice, (P1, K1, P1, K2) 3 times, (P1, K1) 4 (6: 7: 9: 11: 14) times, K1 (0: 1: 1: 0: 0).
These 2 rows form rib.
Work in rib for a further 19 rows, ending with a **RS** row.
Row 22 (WS): Rib 12 (15: 18: 22: 25: 31), inc in next st, rib 4, inc in next st, rib 6, inc in next st, rib 8, inc in next st, rib 4, inc in next st, rib 35, inc in next st, rib 4, inc in next st, rib 8, inc in next st, rib 6, inc in next st, rib 4, inc in next st, rib 12 (15: 18: 22: 25: 31).
123 (129: 135: 143: 149: 161) sts.
Change to 3¼mm (US 3) needles.
Beg and ending rows as indicated and repeating the 24 and 36 row patt repeats throughout, cont in patt from chart for body as follows:
(**Note:** For central 24 row patt repeat, work chart rows 1 and 2 **once only** and then repeat chart rows 3 to 26 **throughout**.)
Cont straight until back measures 32 (32: 33: 33: 33: 33) cm, ending with a WS row.

Shape armholes
Keeping patt correct, cast off 5 (5: 6: 6: 7: 7) sts at beg of next 2 rows.
113 (119: 123: 131: 135: 147) sts.
Dec 1 st at each end of next 1 (3: 3: 5: 5: 7) rows, then on foll 2 (2: 3: 3: 4: 6) alt rows, then on foll 4th row.
105 (107: 109: 113: 115: 119) sts.
Cont straight until armhole measures 17 (18: 18: 19: 20: 21) cm, ending with a WS row.

Shape shoulders and back neck
Cast off 9 (9: 9: 10: 10: 11) sts at beg of next 2 rows.
87 (89: 91: 93: 95: 97) sts.
Next row (RS): Cast off 9 (9: 9: 10: 10: 11) sts, patt until there are 13 (13: 14: 13: 14: 14) sts on right needle and turn, leaving rem sts on a holder.
Work each side of neck separately.
Cast off 4 sts at beg of next row.
Cast off rem 9 (9: 10: 9: 10: 10) sts.
With RS facing, rejoin yarn to rem sts, cast off centre 43 (45: 45: 47: 47: 47) sts, patt to end.
Complete to match first side, reversing shapings.

FRONT
Work as given for back until 24 (24: 24: 28: 28: 28) rows less have been worked than on back to start of shoulder shaping, ending with a WS row.

Shape front neck
Next row (RS): Patt 38 (38: 39: 41: 42: 44) sts and turn, leaving rem sts on a holder.
Work each side of neck separately.
Keeping patt correct, dec 1 st at neck edge of next 6 rows, then on foll 3 alt rows, then on 2 (2: 2: 3: 3: 3) foll 4th rows.
27 (27: 28: 29: 30: 32) sts.
Work 3 rows, ending with a WS row.

Shape shoulder
Cast off 9 (9: 9: 10: 10: 11) sts at beg of next and foll alt row.
Work 1 row.
Cast off rem 9 (9: 10: 9: 10: 10) sts.
With RS facing, rejoin yarn to rem sts, cast off centre 29 (31: 31: 31: 31: 31) sts, patt to end.
Complete to match first side, reversing shapings.

SLEEVES (both alike)
Cast on 71 (73: 75: 79: 81: 83) sts using 2¾mm (US 2) needles.
Row 1 (RS): P0 (1: 0: 0: 1: 0), (P1, K1 tbl) 3 (3: 4: 5: 5: 6) times, (P2, K1 tbl, P1, K1 tbl) 3 times, (P1, K1 tbl) 3 times, (P2, K1 tbl, P1, K1 tbl) 4 times, P1, K1 tbl, P1, (K1 tbl, P1, K1 tbl, P2) 3 times, (K1 tbl, P1) 3 (3: 4: 5: 5: 6) times, P0 (1: 0: 0: 1: 0).
Row 2: K0 (1: 0: 0: 1: 0), (K1, P1) 3 (3: 4: 5: 5: 6) times, (K2, P1, K1, P1) 3 times, (K1, P1) 3 times, (K2, P1, K1, P1) 4 times, K1, P1, K1, (P1, K1, P1, K2) 3 times, (P1, K1) 3 (3: 4: 5: 5: 6) times, K0 (1: 0: 0: 1: 0).

Key

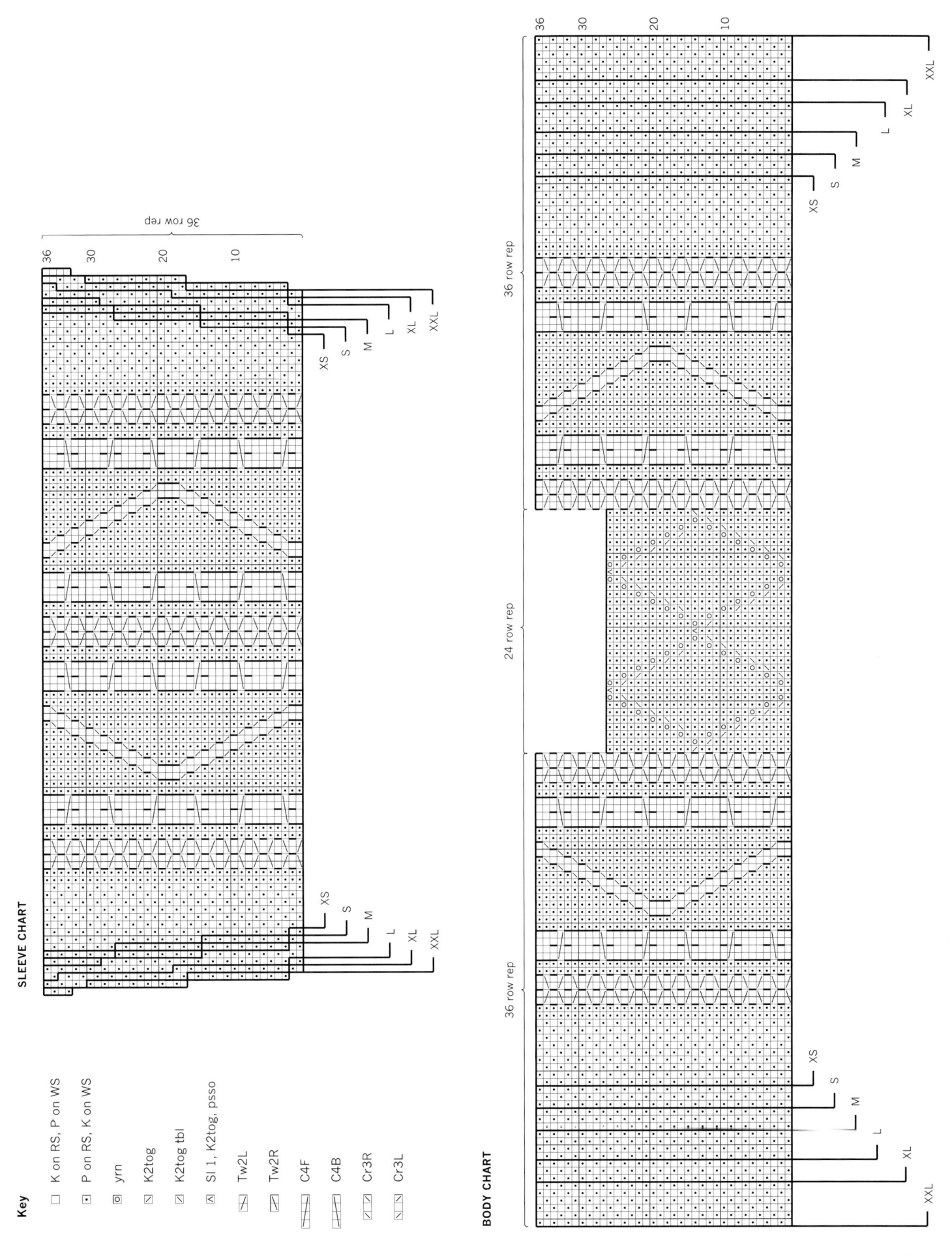

- ☐ K on RS, P on WS
- · P on RS, K on WS
- ◉ yrn
- ╱ K2tog
- ╲ K2tog tbl
- ▲ Sl 1, K2tog, psso
- ╱ Tw2L
- ╲ Tw2R
- C4F
- C4B
- Cr3R
- Cr3L

SLEEVE CHART

36 row rep

BODY CHART

36 row rep

24 row rep

36 row rep

These 2 rows form rib.
Work in rib for a further 23 rows, ending with a **RS** row.
Row 26 (WS): Rib 8 (9: 10: 12: 13: 14), inc in next st, rib 4, inc in next st, rib 6, inc in next st, rib 8, inc in next st, rib 4, inc in next st, rib 5, inc in next st, rib 8, inc in next st, rib 6, inc in next st, rib 4, inc in next st, rib 9 (10: 11: 13: 14: 15). 80 (82: 84: 88: 90: 92) sts.
Change to 3¼mm (US 3) needles.
Beg and ending rows as indicated and repeating the 36 row patt repeat throughout, cont in patt from chart for sleeve as follows:
Work 2 rows, ending with a WS row.
Inc 1 st at each end of next and every foll 12th (12th: 12th: 16th: 14th: 14th) row to 92 (90: 88: 94: 98: 96) sts, then on every foll 14th (14th: 14th: 18th: 16th: 16th) row until there are 94 (96: 98: 100: 104: 106) sts, taking inc sts into moss st.
Cont straight until sleeve measures 32 (33: 34: 35: 36: 37) cm, ending with a WS row.
Shape top
Keeping patt correct, cast off 5 (5: 6: 6: 7: 7) sts at beg of next 2 rows.
84 (86: 86: 88: 90: 92) sts.
Dec 1 st at each end of next 3 rows, then on foll 3 alt rows, then on 4 foll 4th rows.
64 (66: 66: 68: 70: 72) sts.
Work 1 row.

Dec 1 st at each end of next and every foll alt row until 58 sts rem, then on foll 7 rows, ending with a WS row.
Cast off rem 44 sts.

MAKING UP
Press all pieces with a warm iron over a damp cloth.
Join right shoulder seam using back stitch or mattress stitch if preferred.
Neckband
With RS facing and using 2¾mm (US 2) needles, pick up and knit 22 (22: 22: 25: 25: 25) sts down left side of front neck, 29 (31: 31: 31: 31: 31) sts from front, 22 (22: 22: 25: 25: 25) sts up right side of front neck, and 48 (50: 50: 52: 52: 52) sts from back.
121 (125: 125: 133: 133: 133) sts.
Row 1 (WS): K1, *P1, K1, rep from * to end.
Row 2: P1, *K1 tbl, P1, rep from * to end.
Last 2 rows form rib.
Work in rib until neckband measures 2.5 cm from pick-up row, ending with a **RS** row.
Cast off in rib (on **WS**).
Join left shoulder and neckband seam.
Join side seams. Join sleeve seams.
Insert sleeves into armholes.

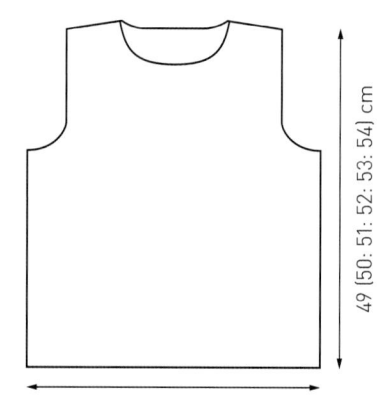

41.5 (44: 46.5: 49: 51.5: 55.5) cm
16¼ (17¼: 18¼: 19¼: 20¼: 21¾) in

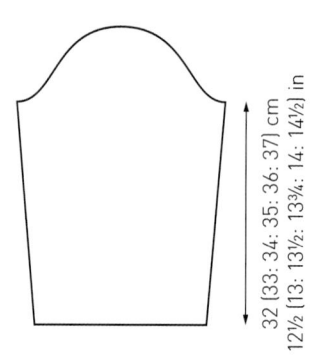

49 (50: 51: 52: 53: 54) cm
19¼ (19¾: 20: 20½: 21: 21¼) in

32 (33: 34: 35: 36: 37) cm
12½ (13: 13½: 13¾: 14: 14½) in

SENTIMENT
Pretty button through sweater

Recommendation
Suitable for the more experienced knitter
Please see pages 14 & 15 for photographs.

	XS	S	M	L	XL	XXL	
To fit bust	81	86	91	97	102	109	cm
	32	34	36	38	40	43	in

Rowan Super Fine Merino 4 ply
7 8 8 9 9 10 x 50gm
Photographed in Marble

Needles
1 pair 2¾mm (no 12) (US 2) needles
1 pair 3¼mm (no 10) (US 3) needles

Buttons – 7

Tension
Based on a stocking stitch tension of 27 sts and 38 rows to 10 cm using 3¼mm (US 3) needles.

Special abbreviations
Tw2L = K into back of second st on left needle, then K first st and slip both sts off left needle together; **Tw2R** = K into front of second st on left needle, then K first st and slip both sts off left needle together.

BACK
Cast on 127 (137: 142: 152: 162: 177) sts using 2¾mm (US 2) needles.
Row 1 (RS): K1, (P1, K1) 3 times, K3, *P2, K3, rep from * to last 7 sts, (K1, P1) 3 times, K1.
Row 2: K1, (P1, K1) 3 times, P3, *K2, P3, rep from * to last 7 sts, (K1, P1) 3 times, K1.
These 2 rows set the sts – 7 sts in moss st at each end of row and all other sts in rib.
Cont as set for a further 22 rows, ending with a WS row.
Row 25 (RS): K1, (P1, K1) 3 times, K3, (P2, K3) 1 (0: 1: 1: 0: 0) times, (P2tog, K3) 20 (24: 23: 25: 29: 32) times, (P2, K3) 1 (0: 1: 1: 0: 0) times, (K1, P1) 3 times, K1.
107 (113: 119: 127: 133: 145) sts.
Keeping sts correct as set (and noting that you will now be working "K1" at top of each dec of previous row), cont as follows:
Row 26: Moss st 7 sts, rib 10 (13: 16: 20: 23: 29), M1, (rib 11, M1) twice, rib 29, (M1, rib 11) twice, M1, rib 10 (13: 16: 20: 23: 29), moss st 7 sts.
113 (119: 125: 133: 139: 151) sts.
Place markers at both ends of last row (to denote top of side seam openings).
Change to 3¼mm (US 3) needles.
Beg and ending rows as indicated and repeating the 16 row patt repeat throughout, cont in patt from chart as follows:
Work 4 (4: 6: 6: 6: 6) rows, ending with a WS row.
Next row (RS): K3, K2tog, patt to last 5 sts, K2tog tbl, K3.
Working all side seam decreases as set by last row, dec 1 st at each end of 8th and foll 8th row, then on 2 foll 6th rows.
103 (109: 115: 123: 129: 141) sts.**
Work 15 (15: 17: 17: 17: 17) rows, ending with a WS row.
Next row (RS): K3, M1, patt to last 3 sts, M1, K3.
Working all side seam increases as set by last row, inc 1 st at each end of 8th and foll 8th row, then on 4 foll 10th rows, taking inc sts into st st.
117 (123: 129: 137: 143: 155) sts.
Cont straight until back measures 38 (38: 39: 39: 39: 39) cm, ending with a WS row.

Shape armholes
Keeping patt correct, cast off 5 (5: 6: 6: 7: 7) sts at beg of next 2 rows.
107 (113: 117: 125: 129: 141) sts.
Dec 1 st at each end of next 1 (3: 3: 5: 5: 7) rows, then on foll 2 (2: 3: 3: 4: 6) alt rows, then on 2 foll 4th rows.
97 (99: 101: 105: 107: 111) sts.
Cont straight until armhole measures 17 (18: 18: 19: 20: 21) cm, ending with a WS row.

Shape shoulders and back neck
Cast off 9 (9: 9: 10: 10: 11) sts at beg of next 2 rows. 79 (81: 83: 85: 87: 89) sts.
Next row (RS): Cast off 9 (9: 9: 10: 10: 11) sts, patt until there are 13 (13: 14: 13: 14: 14) sts on right needle and turn, leaving rem sts on a holder.
Work each side of neck separately.
Cast off 4 sts at beg of next row.
Cast off rem 9 (9: 10: 9: 10: 10) sts.
With RS facing, rejoin yarn to rem sts, cast off centre 35 (37: 37: 39: 39: 39) sts, patt to end.
Complete to match first side, reversing shapings.

FRONT
Work as given for back to **.
Work 1 (1: 3: 3: 3: 3) rows, ending with a WS row.

Divide for front opening
Next row (RS): Patt 48 (51: 54: 58: 61: 67) sts and turn, leaving rem 55 (58: 61: 65: 68: 74) sts on a holder.
Work each side of front separately.
Next row (WS): Cast on 7 sts and work across these 7 sts as follows: K1, (P1, K1) 3 times, then patt to end.
Next row: Patt to last 7 sts, (K1, P1) 3 times, K1.
Last 2 rows set the sts – front opening edge 7 sts in moss st with all other sts still in patt.
55 (58: 61: 65: 68: 74) sts.
Keeping sts correct as now set throughout, cont as follows:
Work 11 rows, ending with a WS row.
Working all side seam increases as set by back, inc 1 st at beg of next and 2 foll 8th rows, then on 4 foll 10th rows, taking inc sts into st st. 62 (65: 68: 72: 75: 81) sts.
Cont straight until front matches back to start of armhole shaping, ending with a WS row.

63

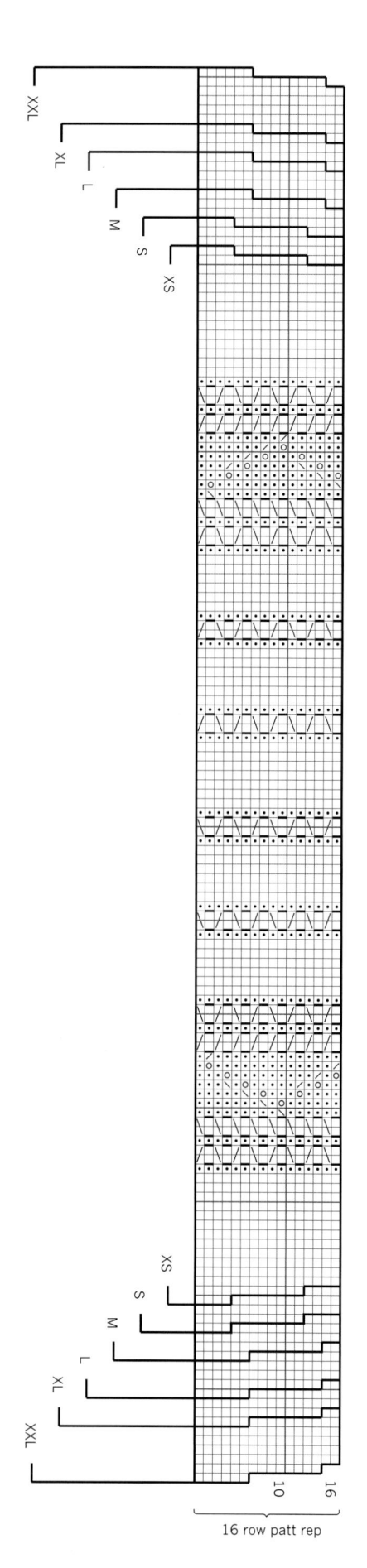

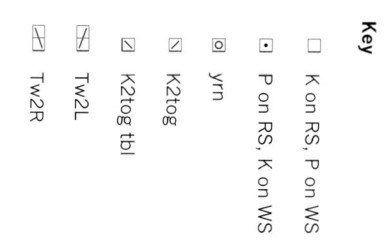

Key
☐ K on RS, P on WS
▪ P on RS, K on WS
○ yrn
╱ K2tog
╲ K2tog tbl
╱╱ Tw2L
╲╲ Tw2R

Shape armhole
Keeping patt correct, cast off 5 (5: 6: 6: 7: 7) sts at beg of next row.
57 (60: 62: 66: 68: 74) sts.
Work 1 row.
Dec 1 st at armhole edge of next 1 (3: 3: 5: 5: 7) rows, then on foll 2 (2: 3: 3: 4: 6) alt rows, then on 2 foll 4th rows.
52 (53: 54: 56: 57: 59) sts.
Cont straight until 24 (24: 24: 28: 28: 28) rows less have been worked than on back to start of shoulder shaping, ending with a WS row.
Shape front neck
Next row (RS): Patt 36 (36: 37: 39: 40: 42) sts and turn, leaving rem 16 (17: 17: 17: 17: 17) sts on another holder (for neckband).
Keeping patt correct, dec 1 st at neck edge of next 4 rows, then on foll 3 alt rows, then on 2 (2: 2: 3: 3: 3) foll 4th rows.
27 (27: 28: 29: 30: 32) sts.
Work 5 rows, ending with a WS row.
Shape shoulder
Cast off 9 (9: 9: 10: 10: 11) sts at beg of next and foll alt row.
Work 1 row.
Cast off rem 9 (9: 10: 9: 10: 10) sts.
Mark positions for 7 buttons along left front opening edge – first button to come in 13th row up from base of front opening, last button to come just above neck shaping, and rem 5 buttons evenly spaced between.
With RS facing, rejoin yarn to 55 (58: 61: 65: 68: 74) sts on first holder and cont as follows:
Next row (RS): K1, (P1, K1) 3 times, patt to end.
Next row: Patt to last 7 sts, (K1, P1) 3 times, K1.
Last 2 rows set the sts – front opening edge 7 sts in moss st with all other sts still in patt.
Keeping sts correct as now set throughout, work 10 rows, ending with a WS row.
Next row (buttonhole row) (RS): K1, P1, K2tog tbl, yfwd (to make a buttonhole), patt to end.

Working a further 5 buttonholes in this way to correspond with positions marked for buttons along left front opening edge, complete to match first side, reversing shapings and working first row of neck shaping as follows:
Shape front neck
Next row (RS): Patt 16 (17: 17: 17: 17: 17) sts and slip these sts onto a holder (for neckband), patt to end.
36 (36: 37: 39: 40: 42) sts.

SLEEVES (both alike)
Cast on 81 (83: 87: 91: 93: 97) sts using 2¾mm (US 2) needles.
Row 1 (RS): K2 (3: 0: 2: 3: 0), P2, *K3, P2, rep from * to last 2 (3: 0: 2: 3: 0) sts, K2 (3: 0: 2: 3: 0).
Row 2: P2 (3: 0: 2: 3: 0), K2, *P3, K2, rep from * to last 2 (3: 0: 2: 3: 0) sts, P2 (3: 0: 2: 3: 0).
These 2 rows form rib.
Work in rib for a further 21 rows, ending with a **RS** row.
Row 24 (WS): P2 (3: 0: 2: 3: 0), K2tog, *P3, K2tog, rep from * to last 2 (3: 0: 2: 3: 0) sts, P2 (3: 0: 2: 3: 0).
65 (67: 69: 73: 75: 77) sts.
Change to 3¼mm (US 3) needles.
Beg with a K row, cont in st st throughout as follows:
Work 2 rows, ending with a WS row.
Working all sleeve increases in same way as side seam increases, inc 1 st at each end of next and every foll 10th (12th: 12th: 14th: 12th: 14th) row to 71 (83: 81: 79: 79: 91) sts, then on every foll 12th (-: 14th: 16th: 14th: 16th) row until there are 81 (-: 85: 87: 91: 93) sts.
Cont straight until sleeve measures 33 (34: 35: 36: 37: 38) cm, ending with a WS row.
Shape top
Cast off 5 (5: 6: 6: 7: 7) sts at beg of next 2 rows. 71 (73: 73: 75: 77: 79) sts.
Dec 1 st at each end of next 3 rows, then on foll alt row, then on 4 foll 4th rows.
55 (57: 57: 59: 61: 63) sts.
Work 1 row.
Dec 1 st at each end of next and every foll alt row until 49 sts rem, then on foll 7 rows, ending with a WS row.
Cast off rem 35 sts.

MAKING UP
Press all pieces with a warm iron over a damp cloth.
Join both shoulder seams using back stitch or mattress stitch if preferred.

16 row patt rep

Neckband
With RS facing and using 2¾mm (US 2) needles, slip 16 (17: 17: 17: 17: 17) sts on right front holder onto right needle, rejoin yarn and pick up and knit 23 (23: 23: 26: 26: 26) sts up right side of neck, 41 (43: 43: 45: 45: 45) sts from back, and 23 (23: 23: 26: 26: 26) sts down left side of neck, then patt across 16 (17: 17: 17: 17: 17) sts on left front holder. 119 (123: 123: 131: 131: 131) sts.
Working all sts in moss st as set by front opening edge sts, work 1 row, ending with a WS row.
Next row (RS): K1, P1, K2tog tbl, yfwd (to make 7th buttonhole), moss st to end.
Work in moss st for a further 6 rows, ending with a **RS** row.
Cast off in moss st (on **WS**).
Join side seams, leaving seams open below markers. Join sleeve seams. Insert sleeves into armholes. At base of front opening, neatly sew cast-on edge in place on inside, then sew on buttons.

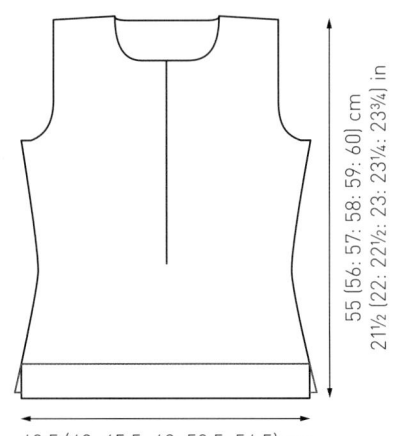

40.5 (43: 45.5: 48: 50.5: 54.5) cm
16 (17: 18: 19: 20: 21½) in

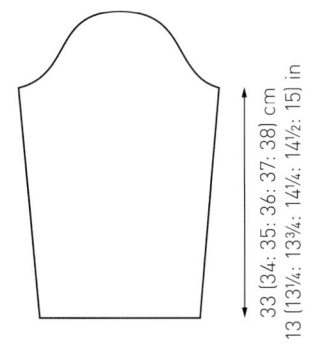

55 (56: 57: 58: 59: 60) cm
21½ (22: 22½: 23: 23¼: 23¾) in

33 (34: 35: 36: 37: 38) cm
13 (13¼: 13¾: 14¼: 14½: 15) in

ADAIR
Understated close-fitting vest

Recommendation
Suitable for the knitter with a little experience
Please see pages 12 & 13 for photographs.

	XS	S	M	L	XL	XXL	
To fit bust	**81**	**86**	**91**	**97**	**102**	**109**	cm
	32	34	36	38	40	43	in

Rowan Alpaca Merino DK

7   7   8   8   9   10 x25gm

Photographed in Ibstock

Needles
1 pair 2¾mm (no 12) (US 2) needles
1 pair 3¼mm (no 10) (US 3) needles

Tension
27 sts and 39 rows to 10 cm measured over stocking stitch using 3¼mm (US 3) needles.

BACK
Cast on 132 (142: 147: 157: 167: 182) sts using 2¾mm (US 2) needles.
Row 1 (RS): K10, *P2, K3, rep from * to last 7 sts, K7.
Row 2: K7, P3, *K2, P3, rep from * to last 7 sts, K7.
These 2 rows set the sts – 7 sts in g st at each end of row and all other sts in rib.
Cont as set for a further 7 rows, ending with a **RS** row.
Row 10 (WS): K7, (P3, K2) 1 (0: 1: 1: 0: 0) times, (P3, K2tog) 21 (25: 24: 26: 30: 33) times, (P3, K2) 1 (0: 1: 1: 0: 0) times, P3, K7.
111 (117: 123: 131: 137: 149) sts.
Change to 3¼mm (US 3) needles.
Row 11 (RS): Knit.
Row 12: K7, P to last 7 sts, K7.
These 2 rows set the sts – 7 sts still in g st at each end of row with all other sts now in st st.
Cont as now set for a further 40 rows, ending with a WS row.
Place markers at both ends of last row (to denote top of side seam openings).
Now working **all** sts in st st, cont as follows:
Cont straight until back measures 33 (33: 34: 34: 34: 34) cm, ending with a WS row.
Shape armholes
Cast off 10 (10: 11: 11: 12: 12) sts at beg of next 2 rows. 91 (97: 101: 109: 113: 125) sts.
Next row (RS): K2tog, K to last 2 sts, K2tog tbl.
Next row: P2tog tbl, P to last 2 sts, P2tog.
Working all armhole decreases as set by last 2 rows, dec 1 st at each end of next 5 (7: 7: 9: 9: 11) rows, then on foll 6 (6: 7: 7: 8: 10) alt rows, then on foll 4th row.
63 (65: 67: 71: 73: 77) sts.
Cont straight until armhole measures 19 (20: 20: 21: 22: 23) cm, ending with a WS row.
Shape back neck
Next row (RS): K14 (14: 15: 16: 17: 19) and turn, leaving rem sts on a holder.
Work each side of neck separately.
Working all neck decreases in same way as armhole decreases, dec 1 st at neck edge of next 6 rows, then on foll 3 alt rows, then on foll 4th row.
4 (4: 5: 6: 7: 9) sts.
Work 3 rows, ending with a WS row.

Shape shoulder
Cast off rem 4 (4: 5: 6: 7: 9) sts.
With RS facing, rejoin yarn to rem sts, cast off centre 35 (37: 37: 39: 39: 39) sts, K to end.
Complete to match first side, reversing shapings.

FRONT
Work as given for back until 34 (34: 34: 38: 38: 38) rows less have been worked than on back to shoulder cast-off, ending with a WS row.
Shape front neck
Next row (RS): K16 (16: 17: 19: 20: 22) and turn, leaving rem sts on a holder.
Work each side of neck separately.
Working all neck decreases in same way as armhole decreases, dec 1 st at neck edge of next 6 rows, then on foll 4 alt rows, then on 1 (1: 1: 2: 2: 2) foll 4th rows, then on foll 6th row. 4 (4: 5: 6: 7: 9) sts.
Work 9 rows, ending with a WS row.
Shape shoulder
Cast off rem 4 (4: 5: 6: 7: 9) sts.
With RS facing, rejoin yarn to rem sts, cast off centre 31 (33: 33: 33: 33: 33) sts, K to end.
Complete to match first side, reversing shapings.

MAKING UP
Press all pieces with a warm iron over a damp cloth.
Join right shoulder seam using back stitch or mattress stitch if preferred.
Neckband
With RS facing and using 2¾mm (US 2) needles, pick up and knit 30 (31: 31: 32: 32: 32) sts down left side of front neck, 31 (33: 33: 33: 33: 33) sts from front, 30 (30: 30: 32: 32: 32) sts up right side of front neck, 18 sts down right side of back neck, 35 (37: 37: 39: 39: 39) sts from back, and 18 sts up left side of back neck.
162 (167: 167: 172: 172: 172) sts.
Row 1 (WS): K2, *P3, K2, rep from * to end.
Row 2: P2, *K3, P2, rep from * to end.
Last 2 rows form rib.
Work in rib for a further 8 rows, ending with a **RS** row.
Cast off in rib (on **WS**).

Continued on next page...

PALE
Pretty garter stitch scarf with eyelet detail

Finished size
Completed scarf is 38 cm (15 in) wide and approx 240 cm (94½ in) long.

Special note: We found it preferable to knit the two yarns together from separate balls rather than winding them together.

SCARF
Cast on 57 sts using 5½mm (US 9) needles and one strand each of yarns A and B held together.
Row 1 (RS): Knit.
Row 2: Knit.
Row 3: Cast on 1 st, then cast off this st and K until there are 7 sts on right needle, yfwd, K2tog, K to last 9 sts, K2tog tbl, yfwd, K7.
Row 4: Cast on 1 st, then cast off this st and K to end.
These 4 rows form patt.
Cont in patt until scarf measures approx 240 cm, ending after patt row 1 and with a **RS** row.
Cast off knitwise (on **WS**).

MAKING UP
Do NOT press.

Recommendation
Suitable for the novice knitter
Please see pages 42 & 43 for photographs.

Rowan Kidsilk Haze and Fine Lace
A Kidsilk Haze   4   x 25gm
B Fine Lace   2   x 50gm
Photographed in Kidsilk Haze in Pearl with Fine Lace in White

Needles
1 pair 5½mm (no 5) (US 9) needles

Tension
15 sts and 26 rows to 10 cm measured over garter stitch using 5½mm (US 9) needles and one strand each of Kidsilk Haze and Fine Lace held together.

ADAIR – Continued from previous page.

Join left shoulder and neckband seam.
Armhole borders (both alike)
With RS facing and using 2¾mm (US 2) needles, pick up and knit 162 (167: 167: 172: 182: 187) sts evenly all round armhole edge.
Beg with row 1, work in rib as given for neckband for 10 rows, ending with a **RS** row.
Cast off in rib (on **WS**).
Join side and armhole border seams, leaving side seams open below markers.

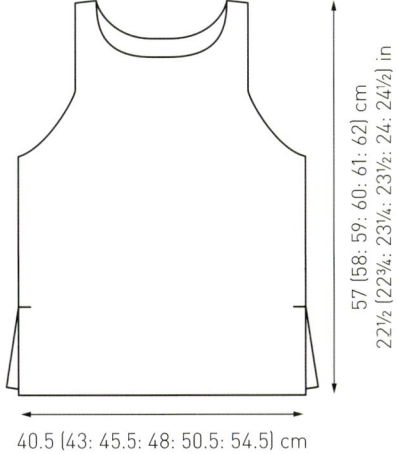

40.5 (43: 45.5: 48: 50.5: 54.5) cm
16 (17: 18: 19: 20: 21½) in

57 (58: 59: 60: 61: 62) cm
22½ (22¾: 23¼: 23½: 24: 24½) in

BLACKENED
Tunic with deep side vents & flared cuffs

Recommendation
Suitable for the novice knitter
Please see pages 18 & 19 for photographs.

	XS	S	M	L	XL	XXL	
To fit bust	**81**	**86**	**91**	**97**	**102**	**109**	cm
	32	34	36	38	40	43	in

Rowan Brushed Fleece

6   7   8   8   9   9 x 50gm
Photographed in Peat

Needles
1 pair 6mm (no 4) (US 10) needles
1 pair 7mm (no 2) (US 10½) needles

Tension
12½ sts and 19 rows to 10 cm measured over stocking stitch using 7mm (US 10½) needles.

BACK
Cast on 53 (57: 61: 63: 67: 71) sts using 7mm (US 10½) needles.
Row 1 (RS): Knit.
Row 2: K5, P to last 5 sts, K5.
Rep last 2 rows until back measures 23 cm, ending with a WS row.
Place markers at both ends of last row (to denote top of side seam openings).
Now working all sts in st st, beg with a K row, cont as follows:
Work 2 rows, ending with a WS row.
Next row (RS): K3, K2tog, K to last 5 sts, K2tog tbl, K3.
Working all side seam decreases as set by last row, dec 1 st at each end of 8th and foll 6th row. 47 (51: 55: 57: 61: 65) sts.
Work 13 rows, ending with a WS row.
Next row (RS): K3, M1, K to last 3 sts, M1, K3.
Working all side seam increases as set by last row, inc 1 st at each end of 8th and foll 8th row. 53 (57: 61: 63: 67: 71) sts.
Cont straight until back measures 53 (53: 54: 54: 54: 54) cm, ending with a WS row.
Shape armholes
Cast off 3 sts at beg of next 2 rows.
47 (51: 55: 57: 61: 65) sts.
Dec 1 st at each end of next 1 (1: 1: 3: 3: 3) rows, then on foll 0 (1: 2: 1: 2: 3) alt rows, then on foll 4th row.
43 (45: 47: 47: 49: 51) sts.
Cont straight until armhole measures 18 (19: 19: 20: 21: 22) cm, ending with a WS row.
Shape shoulders and back neck
Next row (RS): Cast off 3 (3: 4: 3: 4: 4) sts, K until there are 8 (8: 8: 8: 8: 9) sts on right needle and turn, leaving rem sts on a holder.
Work each side of neck separately.
Cast off 4 sts at beg of next row.
Cast off rem 4 (4: 4: 4: 4: 5) sts.
With RS facing, rejoin yarn to rem sts, cast off centre 21 (23: 23: 25: 25: 25) sts, K to end.
Complete to match first side, reversing shapings.

FRONT
Work as given for back until 10 (10: 10: 12: 12: 12) rows less have been worked than on back to start of shoulder shaping, ending with a WS row.

Shape front neck
Next row (RS): K11 (11: 12: 12: 13: 14) and turn, leaving rem sts on a holder.
Work each side of neck separately.
Dec 1 st at neck edge of next 2 rows, then on foll 1 (1: 1: 2: 2: 2) alt rows, then on foll 4th row.
7 (7: 8: 7: 8: 9) sts.
Work 1 row, ending with a WS row.
Shape shoulder
Cast off 3 (3: 4: 3: 4: 4) sts at beg of next row.
Work 1 row.
Cast off rem 4 (4: 4: 4: 4: 5) sts.
With RS facing, rejoin yarn to rem sts, cast off centre 21 (23: 23: 23: 23: 23) sts, K to end.
Complete to match first side, reversing shapings.

SLEEVES (both alike)
Cast on 39 (41: 43: 43: 45: 47) sts using 7mm (US 10½) needles.
Beg with a K row, work in st st throughout as follows:
Work 4 rows, ending with a WS row.
Working all sleeve decreases in same way as side seam decreases, dec 1 st at each end of next and 3 foll 4th rows, then on foll 6th row. 29 (31: 33: 33: 35: 37) sts.
Work 11 rows, ending with a WS row.
Working all sleeve increases in same way as side seam increases, inc 1 st at each end of next and every foll 14th (14th: 22nd: 16th: 24th: 26th) row to 37 (37: 37: 41: 39: 43) sts, then on foll – (16th: 24th: -: 26th: -) row.
37 (39: 39: 41: 41: 43) sts.
Cont straight until sleeve measures 45 (46: 47: 48: 49: 50) cm, ending with a WS row.
Shape top
Cast off 3 sts at beg of next 2 rows.
31 (33: 33: 35: 35: 37) sts.
Dec 1 st at each end of next and 3 foll 4th rows, then on every foll alt row until 19 sts rem, then on foll 3 rows, ending with a WS row.
Cast off rem 13 sts.

MAKING UP
Press all pieces with a warm iron over a damp cloth.
Join right shoulder seam using back stitch or mattress stitch if preferred.

Continued on next page...

KEEPSAKE
Cosy softly cabled scarf

Recommendation
Suitable for the novice knitter
Please see pages 24 & 25 for photographs.

Rowan Kidsilk Haze
5 x 25gm
Photographed in Vanilla

Needles
1 pair 4½mm (no 7) (US 7) needles
1 pair 9mm (no 00) (US 13) needles
Cable needle

Tension
12 sts and 19 rows to 10 cm measured over pattern using a combination of 4½mm (US 7) and 9mm (US 13) needles and 2 strands of yarn held together.

Finished size
Completed scarf is 38 cm (15 in) wide and approx 240 cm (94½ in) long.

SPECIAL ABBREVIATION
C4B = slip next 2 sts onto cable needle and leave at back of work, K2, then K2 from cable needle.

SCARF
Cast on 41 sts using 9mm (US 13) needles and yarn DOUBLE.
Row 1 (WS): Using a 4½mm (US 7) needle, K5, (P1, inc purlwise in next st, P1, K4) 4 times, P1, inc purlwise in next st, P1, K5. 46 sts.
Now work in patt as follows:
Row 1 (RS): Using a 9mm (US 13) needle, K4, P1, (K4, P4) 4 times, K4, P1, K4.
Row 2: Using a 4½mm (US 7) needle, K5, (P4, K4) 5 times, K1.
Rows 3 to 6: As rows 1 and 2, twice.
Row 7: Using a 9mm (US 13) needle, K4, P1, (C4B, P4) 4 times, C4B, P1, K4.
Row 8: As row 2.
These 8 rows form patt.

Cont in patt until scarf measures approx 240 cm, ending after patt row 5 and with a **RS** row.
Next row (WS): Using a 4½mm (US 7) needle, K5, (P1, P2tog, P1, K4) 5 times, K1. 41 sts.
Cast off using a 9mm (US 13) needle.

MAKING UP
Do NOT press.

BLACKENED – *Continued from previous page.*

Collar
With RS facing and using 6mm (US 10) needles, pick up and knit 13 (13: 13: 15: 15: 15) sts down left side of front neck, 21 (23: 23: 23: 23: 23) sts from front, 13 (13: 13: 15: 15: 15) sts up right side of front neck, and 30 (33: 33: 34: 34: 34) sts from back. 77 (82: 82: 87: 87: 87) sts.
Row 1 (WS): K2, *P3, K2, rep from * to end.
Row 2: P2, *K3, P2, rep from * to end.
Last 2 rows form rib.
Cont in rib until collar measures 10 cm from pick-up row, ending with a **RS** row.
Cast off in rib (on **WS**).
Join left shoulder and collar seam. Join side seams, leaving side seams open below markers. Join sleeve seams. Insert sleeves into armholes.

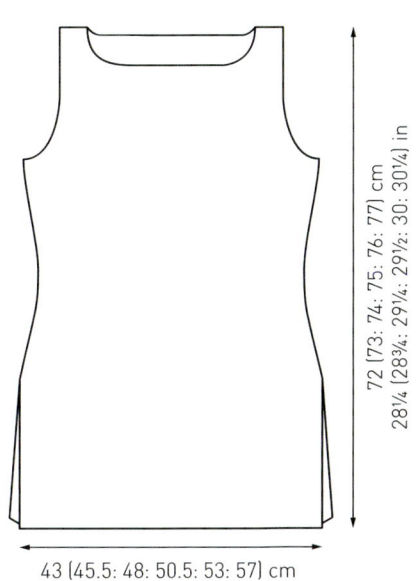

72 (73: 74: 75: 76: 77) cm
28¼ (28¾: 29¼: 29½: 30: 30¼) in

45 (46: 47: 48: 49: 50) cm
17¾ (18: 18½: 19: 19¼: 19¾) in

43 (45.5: 48: 50.5: 53: 57) cm
17 (18: 19: 20: 21: 22½) in

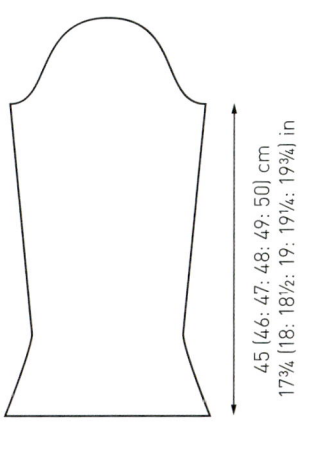

EMMA
Cropped aran cardigan

Recommendation
Suitable for the knitter with a little experience
Please see pages 20 & 21 for photographs.

	XS	S	M	L	XL	XXL	
To fit bust	81	86	91	97	102	109	cm
	32	34	36	38	40	43	in

Rowan Big Wool

7   8   8   9   10   11 x100gm

Photographed in Cactus

Needles
1 pair 7mm (no 2) (US 10½) needles
1 pair 8mm (no 0) (US 11) needles
Cable needle

Buttons – 5

Tension
11 sts and 15 rows to 10 cm measured over stocking stitch using 8mm (US 11) needles.

Pattern note: When casting off across top of cables, dec sts to ensure the edge does not stretch too much. These decreased sts are NOT included in any st counts.

Special abbreviations
C4B = slip next 2 sts onto cn and leave at back of work, K2, then K2 from cn; **C4F** = slip next 2 sts onto cn and leave at front of work, K2, then K2 from cn; **cn** = cable needle; **Cr3L** = slip next 2 sts onto cn and leave at front of work, P1, then K2 from cn; **Cr3R** = slip next st onto cn and leave at back of work, K2, then P1 from cn; **Tw2L** = K into back of second st on left needle, then K first st and slip both sts off left needle together; **Tw2R** = K into front of second st on left needle, then K first st and slip both sts off left needle together.

BACK
Cast on 51 (53: 55: 59: 61: 65) sts using 7mm (US 10½) needles.
Row 1 (RS): P2 (1: 2: 2: 1: 1), *K1 tbl, P1, rep from * to last 1 (0: 1: 1: 0: 0) st, P1 (0: 1: 1: 0: 0).
Row 2: K2 (1: 2: 2: 1: 1), *P1, K1, rep from * to last 1 (0: 1: 1: 0: 0) st, K1 (0: 1: 1: 0: 0).
These 2 rows form rib.
Work in rib for a further 5 rows, ending with a **RS** row.
Row 8 (WS): Rib 7 (8: 9: 11: 12: 14), (M1, rib 4) twice, M1, rib 6, M1, rib 9, M1, rib 6, M1, (rib 4, M1) twice, rib 7 (8: 9: 11: 12: 14). 59 (61: 63: 67: 69: 73) sts.
Change to 8mm (US 11) needles.
Beg and ending rows as indicated and repeating the 12 and 20 row patt repeats throughout, cont in patt from chart for body as follows:
Cont straight until back measures 28 (28: 29: 29: 29: 29) cm, ending with a WS row.
Shape armholes
Keeping patt correct, cast off 2 sts at beg of next 2 rows. 55 (57: 59: 63: 65: 69) sts.
Dec 1 st at each end of next 1 (1: 1: 3: 3: 3) rows, then on foll 2 (2: 2: 2: 2: 4) alt rows. 49 (51: 53: 53: 55: 55) sts.
Cont straight until armhole measures 18 (19: 19: 20: 21: 22) cm, ending with a WS row.
Shape shoulders and back neck
Cast off 5 (6: 6: 6: 6: 6) sts at beg of next 2 rows (see pattern note).
39 (39: 41: 41: 43: 43) sts.
Next row (RS): Cast off 5 (6: 6: 6: 6: 6) sts, patt until there are 10 (9: 10: 9: 10: 10) sts on right needle and turn, leaving rem sts on a holder.
Work each side of neck separately.
Cast off 4 sts at beg of next row.
Cast off rem 6 (5: 6: 5: 6: 6) sts.
With RS facing, rejoin yarn to rem sts, cast off centre 9 (9: 9: 11: 11: 11) sts, patt to end.
Complete to match first side, reversing shapings.

LEFT FRONT
Cast on 29 (30: 31: 33: 34: 36) sts using 7mm (US 10½) needles.
Row 1 (RS): P2 (1: 2: 2: 1: 1), *K1 tbl, P1, rep from * to last 5 sts, K5.
Row 2: K6, *P1, K1, rep from * to last 1 (0: 1: 1: 0: 0) st, K1 (0: 1: 1: 0: 0).
These 2 rows set the sts – front opening edge 5 sts in g st with all other sts in rib.
Cont as set for a further 5 rows, ending with a **RS** row.
Row 8 (WS): Rib 8, M1, rib 6, M1, (rib 4, M1) twice, rib 7 (8: 9: 11: 12: 14). 33 (34: 35: 37: 38: 40) sts.
Change to 8mm (US 11) needles.
Beg and ending rows as indicated, cont in patt from chart for body as follows:
Row 9 (RS): Work first 28 (29: 30: 32: 33: 35) sts as row 1 of chart, K5.
Row 10: K5, work rem 28 (29: 30: 32: 33: 35) sts as row 2 of chart.
These 2 rows set the sts for rest of left front – front opening edge 5 sts still in g st but all other sts now in patt from chart.
Cont as now set until left front matches back to start of armhole shaping, ending with a WS row.
Shape armhole
Keeping patt correct, cast off 2 sts at beg of next row. 31 (32: 33: 35: 36: 38) sts.
Work 1 row.
Dec 1 st at armhole edge of next 1 (1: 1: 3: 3: 3) rows, then on foll 2 (2: 2: 2: 2: 4) alt rows. 28 (29: 30: 30: 31: 31) sts.
Cont straight until 10 (10: 10: 12: 12: 12) rows less have been worked than on back to start of shoulder shaping, ending with a WS row.
Shape front neck
Next row (RS): Patt 20 (21: 22: 22: 23: 23) sts and turn, leaving rem 8 sts on a holder (for neckband).
Keeping patt correct, dec 1 st at neck edge of next 2 rows, then on foll 1 (1: 1: 2: 2: 2) alt rows, then on foll 4th row. 16 (17: 18: 17: 18: 18) sts.
Work 1 row, ending with a WS row.
Shape shoulder
Cast off 5 (6: 6: 6: 6: 6) sts at beg of next and foll alt row (see pattern note).
Work 1 row.
Cast off rem 6 (5: 6: 5: 6: 6) sts.
Mark positions for 5 buttons along left front opening edge – first button to come level with row 9, last button to come just above start of front neck shaping, and rem 3 buttons evenly spaced between.

RIGHT FRONT

Cast on 29 (30: 31: 33: 34: 36) sts using 7mm (US 10½) needles.

Row 1 (RS): K5, P1, *K1 tbl, P1, rep from * to last 1 (0: 1: 1: 0: 0) st, P1 (0: 1: 1: 0: 0).

Row 2: K2 (1: 2: 2: 1: 1), *P1, K1, rep from * to last 5 sts, K5.

These 2 rows set the sts – front opening edge 5 sts in g st with all other sts in rib.
Cont as set for a further 5 rows, end with a **RS** row.

Row 8 (WS): Rib 7 (8: 9: 11: 12: 14), M1, (rib 4, M1) twice, rib 6, M1, rib 8.
33 (34: 35: 37: 38: 40) sts.

Change to 8mm (US 11) needles.
Beg and ending rows as indicated, cont in patt from chart for body as follows:

Row 1 (buttonhole row) (RS): K1, K2tog tbl, yfwd (to make a buttonhole), K2, work rem 28 (29: 30: 32: 33: 35) sts as row 1 of chart.

Making a further 3 buttonholes in this way to correspond with positions marked on left front for buttons and noting that no further reference will be made to buttonholes, cont as follows:

Row 2: Work first 28 (29: 30: 32: 33: 35) sts as row 2 of chart, K5.

These 2 rows set the sts for rest of right front – front opening edge 5 sts still in g st but all other sts now in patt from chart.
Complete to match left front, reversing shapings and working first row of neck shaping as follows:

Shape front neck

Next row (RS): Patt 8 sts and slip these sts onto a holder (for neckband), patt to end. 20 (21: 22: 22: 23: 23) sts.

Key

- ☐ K on RS, P on WS
- ⊡ P on RS, K on WS
- Tw2L
- Tw2R
- C4F
- C4B
- Cr3R
- Cr3L

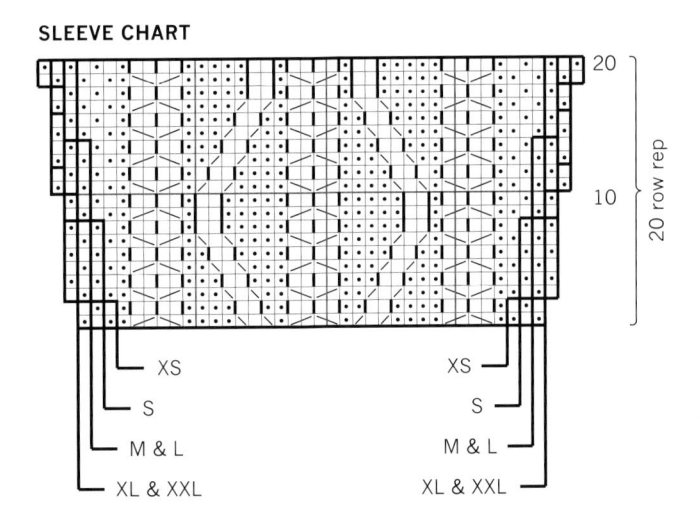

SLEEVE CHART

BODY CHART

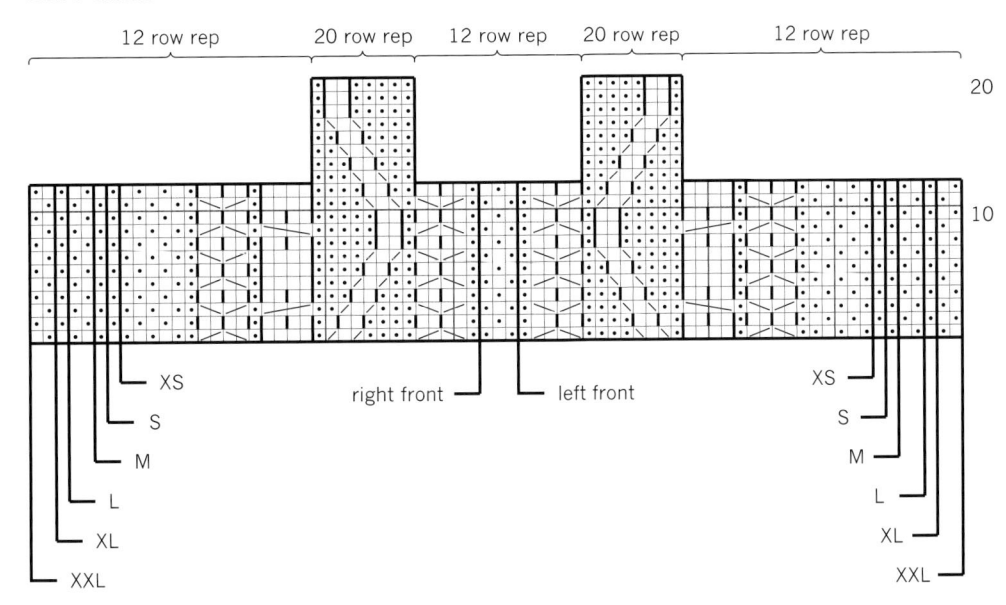

SLEEVES (both alike)
Cast on 25 (27: 29: 29: 31: 31) sts using 7mm (US 10½) needles.
Row 1 (RS): P1 (2: 1: 1: 2: 2), *K1 tbl, P1, rep from * to last 0 (1: 0: 0: 1: 1) st, P0 (1: 0: 0: 1: 1).
Row 2: K1 (2: 1: 1: 2: 2), *P1, K1, rep from * to last 0 (1: 0: 0: 1: 1) st, K0 (1: 0: 0: 1: 1).
These 2 rows form rib.
Work in rib for a further 7 rows, ending with a **RS** row.
Row 10 (WS): Rib 2 (3: 4: 4: 5: 5), M1, rib 4, M1, rib 7, M1, rib 6, M1, rib 4, M1, rib 2 (3: 4: 4: 5: 5).
30 (32: 34: 34: 36: 36) sts.
Change to 8mm (US 11) needles.
Beg and ending rows as indicated and repeating the 20 row patt repeat throughout, cont in patt from chart for sleeve as follows:
Inc 1 st at each end of 3rd and every foll 6th (6th: 8th: 6th: 10th: 8th) row to 38 (40: 40: 38: 46: 48) sts, then on every foll 8th (8th: 10th: 8th: -: -) row until there are 42 (44: 44: 46: -: -) sts, taking inc sts into moss st.
Cont straight until sleeve measures 35 (36: 37: 38: 39: 40) cm, ending with a WS row.
Shape top
Keeping patt correct, cast off 2 sts at beg of next 2 rows.
38 (40: 40: 42: 42: 44) sts.

Dec 1 st at each end of next and every foll alt row until 34 sts rem, then on foll 5 rows, ending with a WS row.
Cast off rem 24 sts (see pattern note).

MAKING UP
Press all pieces with a warm iron over a damp cloth.
Join both shoulder seams using back stitch or mattress stitch if preferred.
Neckband
With RS facing and using 7mm (US 10½) needles, slip 8 sts on right front holder onto right needle, rejoin yarn and pick up and knit 12 (12: 12: 14: 14: 14) sts up right side of neck, 17 (17: 17: 19: 19: 19) sts from back, and 12 (12: 12: 14: 14: 14) sts down left side of neck, then patt across 8 sts on left front holder. 57 (57: 57: 63: 63: 63) sts.
Row 1 (WS): K6, *P1, K1, rep from * to last 5 sts, K5.
Row 2: K1, K2tog tbl, yfwd (to make 5th buttonhole), K2, P1, *K1 tbl, P1, rep from * to last 5 sts, K5.
These 2 rows set the sts – front opening edge 5 sts in g st at each end of row and all other sts in rib.
Cont as set for a further 4 rows, ending with a RS row.
Cast off in patt (on WS).
Join side seams. Join sleeve seams. Insert sleeves into armholes. Sew on buttons.

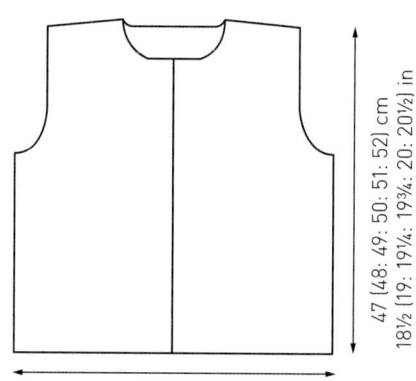

45.5 (48: 50.5: 53: 55.5: 59.5) cm
18 (19: 20: 21: 22: 23½) in

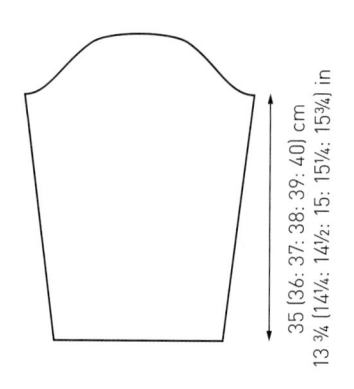

47 (48: 49: 50: 51: 52) cm
18½ (19: 19¼: 19¾: 20: 20½) in

35 (36: 37: 38: 39: 40) cm
13¾ (14¼: 14½: 15: 15¼: 15¾) in

ARGYLE
Patterned cardigan worked in soft natural shades

Recommendation
Suitable for the more experienced knitter
Please see pages 22 & 23 for photographs.

	XS	S	M	L	XL	XXL	
To fit bust	81	86	91	97	102	109	cm
	32	34	36	38	40	43	in

Rowan Brushed Fleece and Kidsilk Haze
A Brushed Fleece Cairn
    6   6   7   7   8   9 x 50gm
B Brushed Fleece Crag
    4   4   4   5   5   6 x 50gm
C Kidsilk Haze Drab
    2   2   2   3   3   3 x 25gm

Needles
1 pair 5mm (no 6) (US 8) needles
1 pair 6mm (no 4) (US 10) needles

Buttons – 6

Tension
14 sts and 21 rows to 10 cm measured over stocking stitch using 6mm (US 10) needles and Brushed Fleece.

BACK
Cast on 88 (94: 98: 104: 108: 114) sts using 5mm (US 8) needles and yarn A.
Row 1 (RS): K3 (1: 3: 1: 3: 1), P2, *K3, P2, rep from * to last 3 (1: 3: 1: 3: 1) sts, K3 (1: 3: 1: 3: 1).
Row 2: P3 (1: 3: 1: 3: 1), K2, *P3, K2, rep from * to last 3 (1: 3: 1: 3: 1) sts, P3 (1: 3: 1: 3: 1).
These 2 rows form rib.
Work in rib for a further 9 rows, ending with a **RS** row.
Row 12 (WS): P3 (1: 3: 1: 3: 1), K2tog, *P3, K2tog, rep from * to last 3 (1: 3: 1: 3: 1) sts, P3 (1: 3: 1: 3: 1).
71 (75: 79: 83: 87: 91) sts.
Change to 6mm (US 10) needles.
Beg and ending rows as **indicated**, using the intarsia technique and repeating the 32 row patt repeat throughout, cont in patt from chart, which is worked entirely in st st beg with a K row, as follows:
Cont straight until back measures 49 (49: 50: 50: 50: 50) cm, ending with a WS row.
Shape armholes
Keeping patt correct, cast off 4 sts at beg of next 2 rows.
63 (67: 71: 75: 79: 83) sts.
Dec 1 st at each end of next 3 (3: 5: 5: 7: 7) rows, then on foll 2 (3: 2: 4: 3: 4) alt rows, then on foll 4th row.
51 (53: 55: 55: 57: 59) sts.
Cont straight until armhole measures 19 (20: 20: 21: 22: 23) cm, ending with a WS row.
Shape shoulders and back neck
Cast off 5 (5: 6: 5: 6: 6) sts at beg of next 2 rows. 41 (43: 43: 45: 45: 47) sts.
Next row (RS): Cast off 5 (5: 6: 5: 6: 6) sts, patt until there are 9 (10: 9: 10: 9: 10) sts on right needle and turn, leaving rem sts on a holder.
Work each side of neck separately.
Cast off 4 sts at beg of next row.
Cast off rem 5 (6: 5: 6: 5: 6) sts.
With RS facing, rejoin yarns to rem sts, cast off centre 13 (13: 13: 15: 15: 15) sts, patt to end.
Complete to match first side, reversing shapings.

LEFT FRONT
Cast on 50 (53: 55: 58: 60: 63) sts using 5mm (US 8) needles and yarn A.
Row 1 (RS): K3 (1: 3: 1: 3: 1), P2, *K3, P2, rep from * to last 5 sts, (K1, P1) twice, K1.
Row 2: K1, (P1, K1) twice, K2, *P3, K2, rep from * to last 3 (1: 3: 1: 3: 1) sts, P3 (1: 3: 1: 3: 1).
These 2 rows set the sts – front opening edge 5 sts in moss st with all other sts in rib.
Cont as set for a further 9 rows, ending with a **RS** row.
Row 12 (WS): K1, (P1, K1) twice, K2tog, *P3, K2tog, rep from * to last 3 (1: 3: 1: 3: 1) sts, P3 (1: 3: 1: 3: 1). 41 (43: 45: 47: 49: 51) sts.
Change to 6mm (US 10) needles.
Beg and ending rows as indicated, now place chart as follows:
Row 13 (RS): Patt first 36 (38: 40: 42: 44: 46) sts as row 1 of chart, using yarn A moss st 5 sts.
Row 14: Using yarn A moss st 5 sts, patt rem 36 (38: 40: 42: 44: 46) sts as row 2 of chart.
These 2 rows set the sts for rest of left front – front opening edge 5 sts still in moss st using yarn A and all other sts now in patt from chart.
Keeping sts correct as now set throughout, cont as follows:
Cont straight until 22 rows less have been worked than on back to start of armhole shaping, ending with a WS row.
Shape front slope
Next row (RS): Patt to last 7 sts, K2tog tbl, using yarn A moss st 5 sts.
Working all front slope decreases as set by last row, dec 1 st at front slope edge of 4th and 2 (1: 1: 3: 2: 1) foll 4th rows, then on 1 (2: 2: 0: 1: 2) foll 6th rows. 36 (38: 40: 42: 44: 46) sts.
Work 3 (1: 1: 5: 3: 1) rows, ending with a WS row.
Shape armhole
Keeping patt correct, cast off 4 sts at beg and dec 0 (0: 0: 1: 0: 0) st at end of next row. 32 (34: 36: 37: 40: 42) sts.
Work 1 row.
Dec 1 st at armhole edge of next 3 (3: 5: 5: 7: 7) rows, then on foll 2 (3: 2: 4: 3: 4) alt rows, then on foll 4th row **and at same time** dec 1 st at front slope edge of next (3rd: 3rd: 5th: next: 3rd) and 1 (1: 1: 2: 2: 2) foll 6th rows.
24 (25: 26: 24: 26: 27) sts.

Dec 1 st at front slope edge **only** on 2nd (2nd: 2nd: 6th: 2nd: 2nd) and 3 (3: 3: 2: 3: 3) foll 6th rows.
20 (21: 22: 21: 22: 23) sts.
Cont straight until left front matches back to start of shoulder shaping, ending with a WS row.

Shape shoulder
Cast off 5 (5: 6: 5: 6: 6) sts at beg of next and foll alt row, then 5 (6: 5: 6: 5: 6) sts at beg of foll alt row. 5 sts.
Inc 1 st at end of next row. 6 sts.
Cont in moss st on these 6 sts only (for back neck border extension) until this strip measures 7.5 (7.5: 7.5: 8: 8: 8) cm, ending with a WS row.
Cast off.
Mark positions for 6 buttons along left front opening edge – first button to come level with row 3, second button to come level with row 13, last button to come 2 cm below start of front slope shaping, and rem 3 buttons evenly spaced between.

RIGHT FRONT
Cast on 50 (53: 55: 58: 60: 63) sts using 5mm (US 8) needles and yarn A.

Row 1 (RS): K1, (P1, K1) twice, P2, *K3, P2, rep from * to last 3 (1: 3: 1: 3: 1) sts, K3 (1: 3: 1: 3: 1).
Row 2: P3 (1: 3: 1: 3: 1), K2, *P3, K2, rep from * to last 5 sts, (K1, P1) twice, K1.
These 2 rows set the sts – front opening edge 5 sts in moss st with all other sts in rib.
Row 3 (buttonhole row): K1, P2tog, yrn (to make first buttonhole), P1, K1, rib to end.
Cont as set for a further 8 rows, ending with a **RS** row.
Row 12 (WS): P3 (1: 3: 1: 3: 1), K2tog, *P3, K2tog, rep from * to last 5 sts, (K1, P1) twice, K1. 41 (43: 45: 47: 49: 51) sts.
Change to 6mm (US 10) needles.
Beg and ending rows as indicated, now place chart as follows:
Row 13 (buttonhole row) (RS): Using yarn A K1, P2tog, yrn (to make second buttonhole), P1, K1, patt rem 36 (38: 40: 42: 44: 46) sts as row 1 of chart.
Making a further 4 buttonholes in this way to correspond with positions marked on left front for buttons and noting that no further reference will be made to buttonholes, cont as follows:
Row 14: Patt first 36 (38: 40: 42: 44: 46) sts as row 2 of chart, using yarn A moss st 5 sts.

These 2 rows set the sts for rest of right front – front opening edge 5 sts still in moss st using yarn A and all other sts now in patt from chart.
Keeping sts correct as now set throughout, cont as follows:
Cont straight until 22 rows less have been worked than on back to start of armhole shaping, ending with a WS row.

Shape front slope
Next row (RS): Using yarn A moss st 5 sts, K2tog, patt to end.
Working all front slope decreases as set by last row, complete to match left front, reversing shapings.

SLEEVES (both alike)
Cast on 38 (42: 44: 44: 46: 48) sts using 5mm (US 8) needles and yarn A.
Row 1 (RS): K3 (0: 1: 1: 2: 3), P2, *K3, P2, rep from * to last 3 (0: 1: 1: 2: 3) sts, K3 (0: 1: 1: 2: 3).
Row 2: P3 (0: 1: 1: 2: 3), K2, *P3, K2, rep from * to last 3 (0: 1: 1: 2: 3) sts, P3 (0: 1: 1: 2: 3).
These 2 rows form rib.
Work in rib for a further 7 rows, ending with a **RS** row.

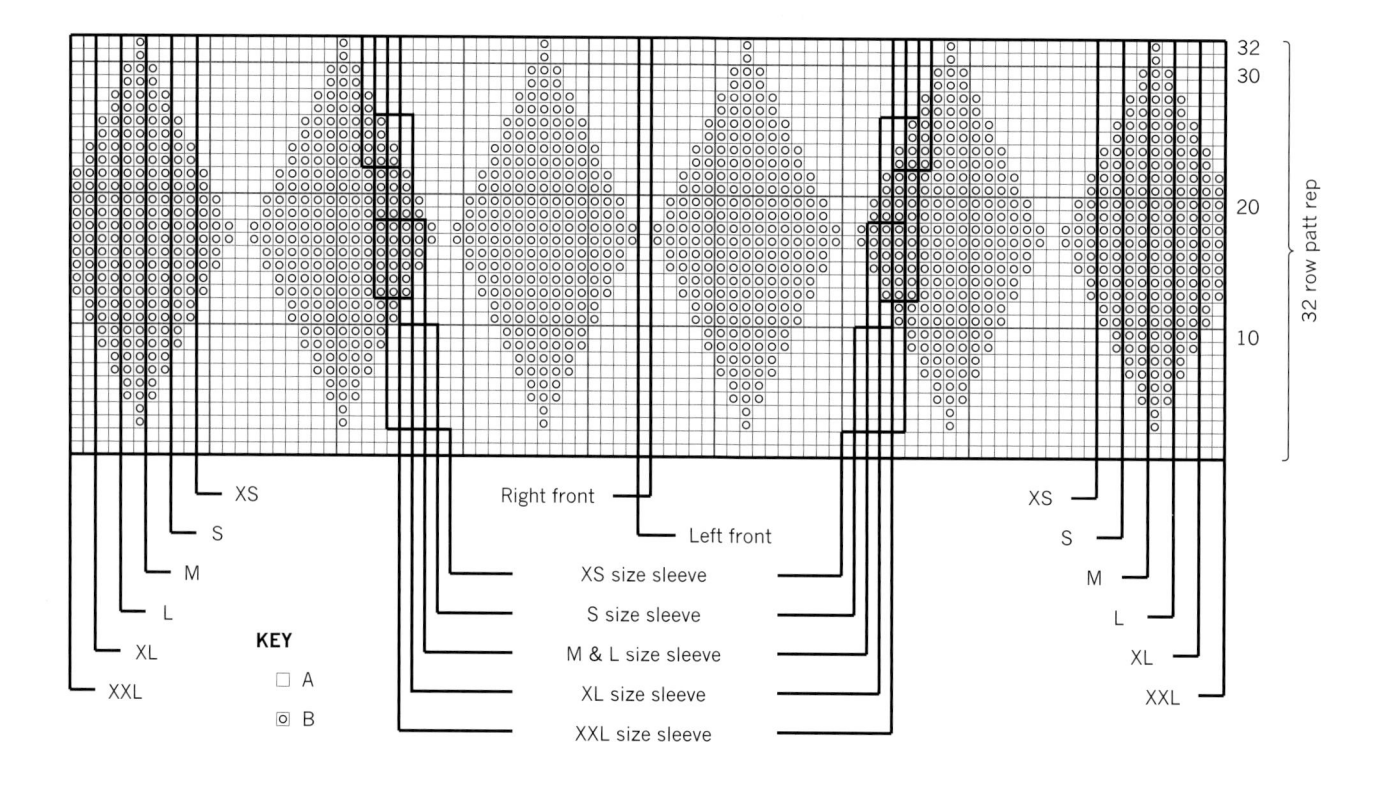

Row 10 (WS): P3 (0: 1: 1: 2: 3), K2tog, *P3, K2tog, rep from * to last 3 (0: 1: 1: 2: 3) sts, P3 (0: 1: 1: 2: 3).
31 (33: 35: 35: 37: 39) sts.
Change to 6mm (US 10) needles.
Beg and ending rows as indicated, cont in patt from chart as follows:
Work 2 rows, ending with a WS row.
Inc 1 st at each end of next and every foll 8th (8th: 10th: 8th: 10th: 10th) row to 47 (47: 53: 45: 51: 51) sts, then on every foll 10th (10th: -: 10th: 12th: 12th) row until there are 51 (53: -: 55: 55: 57) sts, taking inc sts into patt.
Cont straight until sleeve measures 47 (48: 49: 50: 51: 52) cm, ending with a WS row.

Shape top
Keeping patt correct, cast off 4 sts at beg of next 2 rows.
43 (45: 45: 47: 47: 49) sts.
Dec 1 st at each end of next and foll alt row, then on 2 foll 4th rows.
35 (37: 37: 39: 39: 41) sts.
Work 3 rows.
Dec 1 st at each end of next and every foll alt row until 31 sts rem, then on foll 5 rows, ending with a WS row.
Cast off rem 21 sts.

MAKING UP
Press all pieces with a warm iron over a damp cloth.

Swiss darning
Using 3 strands of yarn C held together, thread a blunt darning needle with a length of yarn and using the photograph on page 22 as a guide, swiss darn trellis onto all pieces of work.
Please note: Each swiss darned stitch covers ONE stitch and TWO rows, rather than the conventional way of one stitch and one row.

Working from the bottom of the swiss darning chart below, bring point of needle through from back at base of the stitch to be worked and draw yarn through, leaving an end at the back, take needle behind the 2 loops of the stitch 2 rows above from right to left and draw yarn through, insert needle into same place as before at the base of the first stitch and bring through at base of next stitch to be covered, draw yarn through to the tension of main knitting. Continue in this way, making sure your embroidery matches the knitting tension as too loose a stitch will show the stitch underneath and too tight stitch will make the fabric pucker.

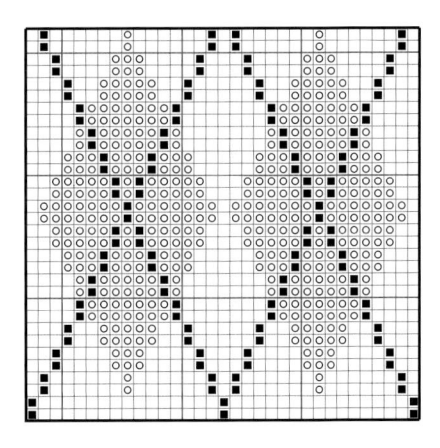

Join both shoulder seams using back stitch or mattress stitch if preferred. Join ends of back neck border extensions, then sew one edge to back neck. Join side seams.
Join sleeve seams.
Insert sleeves into armholes.
Sew on buttons.

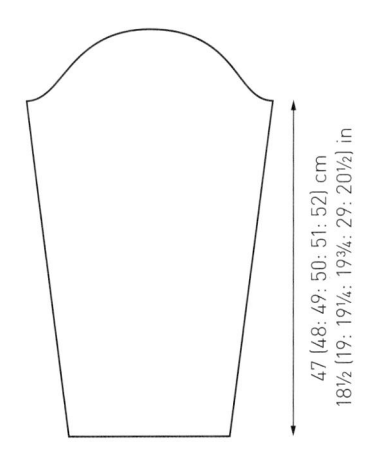

ESCAPE
Neat cardigan worked in eyelet & aran stitches

Recommendation
Suitable for the more experienced knitter
Please see pages 28 & 29 for photographs.

	XS	S	M	L	XL	XXL	
To fit bust	81	86	91	97	102	109	cm
	32	34	36	38	40	43	in

Rowan Super Fine Merino 4 ply
                  8   8   9   9   10   11 x 50gm
Photographed in Marble

Needles
1 pair 2¾mm (no 12) (US 2) needles
1 pair 3¼mm (no 10) (US 3) needles
Cable needle

Buttons – 9

Tension
Based on a stocking stitch tension of 27 sts and 38 rows to 10 cm using 3¼mm (US 3) needles.

Special abbreviations
C4B = slip next 2 sts onto cn and leave at back of work, K2, then K2 from cn; **C4F** = slip next 2 sts onto cn and leave at front of work, K2, then K2 from cn; **cn** = cable needle; **Cr3L** = slip next 2 sts onto cn and leave at front of work, P1, then K2 from cn; **Cr3R** = slip next st onto cn and leave at back of work, K2, then P1 from cn; **Tw2L** = K into back of second st on left needle, then K first st and slip both sts off left needle together; **Tw2R** = K into front of second st on left needle, then K first st and slip both sts off left needle together.

BACK
Cast on 110 (116: 122: 130: 136: 148) sts using 2¾mm (US 2) needles.
Row 1 (RS): P1 (0: 1: 1: 0: 0), (P1, K1 tbl) 4 (6: 7: 9: 11: 14) times, (P2, K1 tbl, P1, K1 tbl) 3 times, (P1, K1 tbl) 3 times, (P1, K1 tbl, P2, K1 tbl) 3 times, (P1, K1 tbl) twice, (P2, K1 tbl, P1, K1 tbl) 3 times, (P1, K1 tbl) twice, (P2, K1 tbl, P1, K1 tbl) 3 times, (P1, K1 tbl) 3 times, (P2, K1 tbl, P1, K1 tbl) 3 times, P1, (K1 tbl, P1) 2 (4: 5: 7: 9: 12) times, P1 (0: 1: 1: 0: 0).
Row 2: K1 (0: 1: 1: 0: 0), (K1, P1) 4 (6: 7: 9: 11: 14) times, (K2, P1, K1, P1) 3 times, (K1, P1) 3 times, (K1, P1, K2, P1) 3 times, (K1, P1) twice, (K2, P1, K1, P1) 3 times, (K1, P1) twice, (K2, P1, K1, P1) 3 times, (K1, P1) 3 times, (K2, P1, K1, P1) 3 times, K1, (P1, K1) 2 (4: 5: 7: 9: 12) times, K1 (0: 1: 1: 0: 0).
These 2 rows form rib.
Work in rib for a further 19 rows, ending with a **RS** row.
Row 22 (WS): Rib 12 (15: 18: 22: 25: 31), inc in next st, rib 4, inc in next st, rib 8, inc in next st, rib 6, inc in next st, rib 4, inc in next st, rib 2, inc in next st, rib 10, inc in next st, rib 4, inc in next st, rib 9, inc in next st, rib 3, inc in next st, rib 4, inc in next st, rib 5, inc in next st, rib 9, inc in next st, rib 4, inc in next st, rib 12 (15: 18: 22: 25: 31).
124 (130: 136: 144: 150: 162) sts.
Change to 3¼mm (US 3) needles.
Beg and ending rows as indicated and repeating the 36 row patt repeat throughout, cont in patt from chart for body as follows:
Cont straight until back measures 30 (30: 31: 31: 31: 31) cm, ending with a WS row.
Shape armholes
Keeping patt correct, cast off 5 (5: 6: 6: 7: 7) sts at beg of next 2 rows.
114 (120: 124: 132: 136: 148) sts.
Dec 1 st at each end of next 1 (3: 3: 5: 5: 7) rows, then on foll 2 (2: 3: 3: 4: 6) alt rows, then on foll 4th row.
106 (108: 110: 114: 116: 120) sts.
Cont straight until armhole measures 17 (18: 18: 19: 20: 21) cm, ending with a WS row.
Shape shoulders and back neck
Cast off 11 (11: 11: 11: 12: 12) sts at beg of next 2 rows.
84 (86: 88: 92: 92: 96) sts.
Next row (RS): Cast off 11 (11: 11: 11: 12: 12) sts, patt until there are 14 (14: 15: 16: 15: 17) sts on right needle and turn, leaving rem sts on a holder.
Work each side of neck separately.
Cast off 4 sts at beg of next row.
Cast off rem 10 (10: 11: 12: 11: 13) sts.
With RS facing, rejoin yarn to rem sts, cast off centre 34 (36: 36: 38: 38: 38) sts, patt to end.
Complete to match first side, reversing shapings.

LEFT FRONT
Cast on 63 (66: 69: 73: 76: 82) sts using 2¾mm (US 2) needles.
Row 1 (RS): P1 (0: 1: 1: 0: 0), (P1, K1 tbl) 4 (6: 7: 9: 11: 14) times, (P2, K1 tbl, P1, K1 tbl) 3 times, (P1, K1 tbl) 3 times, (P1, K1 tbl, P2, K1 tbl) 3 times, (P1, K1 tbl) twice, P2, K1 tbl, P1, K1 tbl, P2, (K1, P1) 3 times, K1.
Row 2: K1, (P1, K1) 3 times, K2, P1, K1, P1, K2, (P1, K1) twice, (P1, K2, P1, K1) 3 times, (P1, K1) 3 times, (P1, K1, P1, K2) 3 times, (P1, K1) 4 (6: 7: 9: 11: 14) times, K1 (0: 1: 1: 0: 0).
These 2 rows set the sts – front opening edge 7 sts in moss st with all other sts in rib.
Cont as set for a further 19 rows, ending with a **RS** row.
Row 22 (WS): Moss st 7 sts, rib 3, inc in next st, rib 9, inc in next st, rib 3, inc in next st, rib 4, inc in next st, rib 5, inc in next st, rib 9, inc in next st, rib 4, inc in next st, rib 12 (15: 18: 22: 25: 31).
70 (73: 76: 80: 83: 89) sts.
Change to 3¼mm (US 3) needles.
Beg and ending rows as indicated and repeating the 36 row patt repeat throughout, cont in patt from chart for body as follows:
Row 1 (RS): Work first 63 (66: 69: 73: 76: 82) sts as row 1 of chart, moss st 7 sts.
Row 2: Moss st 7 sts, work rem 63 (66: 69: 73: 76: 82) sts as row 2 of chart.
These 2 rows set the sts for rest of left front – front opening edge 7 sts still in moss st with all other sts now in patt.
Cont as now set until left front matches back to start of armhole shaping, ending with a WS row.

Shape armhole

Keeping patt correct, cast off 5 (5: 6: 6: 7: 7) sts at beg of next row. 65 (68: 70: 74: 76: 82) sts. Work 1 row.
Dec 1 st at armhole edge of next 1 (3: 3: 5: 5: 7) rows, then on foll 2 (2: 3: 3: 4: 6) alt rows, then on foll 4th row. 61 (62: 63: 65: 66: 68) sts.
Cont straight until 24 (24: 24: 28: 28: 28) rows less have been worked than on back to start of shoulder shaping, ending with a WS row.

Shape front neck

Next row (RS): Patt 43 (43: 44: 46: 47: 49) sts and turn, leaving rem 18 (19: 19: 19: 19: 19) sts on a holder (for neckband).
Keeping patt correct, dec 1 st at neck edge of next 6 rows, then on foll 3 alt rows, then on 2 (2: 2: 3: 3: 3) foll 4th rows.
32 (32: 33: 34: 35: 37) sts.
Work 3 rows, ending with a WS row.

Shape shoulder

Cast off 11 (11: 11: 11: 12: 12) sts at beg of next and foll alt row.
Work 1 row.
Cast off rem 10 (10: 11: 12: 11: 13) sts.
Mark positions for 9 buttons along left front edge – first button to come level with row 5, last button to come just above start of front neck shaping, and rem 7 buttons evenly spaced between.

RIGHT FRONT

Cast on 63 (66: 69: 73: 76: 82) sts using 2¾mm (US 2) needles.
Row 1 (RS): K1, (P1, K1) 3 times, P2, K1 tbl, P1, K1 tbl, P2, (K1 tbl, P1) twice, (K1 tbl, P2, K1 tbl, P1) 3 times, (K1 tbl, P1) 3 times, (K1 tbl, P1, K1 tbl, P2) 3 times, (K1 tbl, P1) 4 (6: 7: 9: 11: 14) times, P1 (0: 1: 1: 0: 0).
Row 2: K1 (0: 1: 1: 0: 0), (K1, P1) 4 (6: 7: 9: 11: 14) times, (K2, P1, K1, P1) 3 times, (K1, P1) 3 times, (K1, P1, K2, P1) 3 times, (K1, P1) twice, K2, P1, K1, P1, K2, (K1, P1) 3 times, K1.
These 2 rows set the sts – front opening edge 7 sts in moss st with all other sts in rib.
Cont as set for a further 2 rows, end with a WS row.
Row 5 (buttonhole row) (RS): K1, P1, K2tog tbl, yfwd (to make first buttonhole), patt to end.
Making a further 7 buttonholes in this way to correspond with positions marked on left front for buttons and noting that no further reference will be made to buttonholes, cont as follows:
Work 16 rows, ending with a RS row.
Row 22 (WS): Rib 12 (15: 18: 22: 25: 31), inc in next st, rib 4, inc in next st, rib 8, inc in next st, rib 6, inc in next st, rib 4, inc in next st, rib 2, inc in next st, rib 10, inc in next st, rib 3, moss st 7 sts. 70 (73: 76: 80: 83: 89) sts.

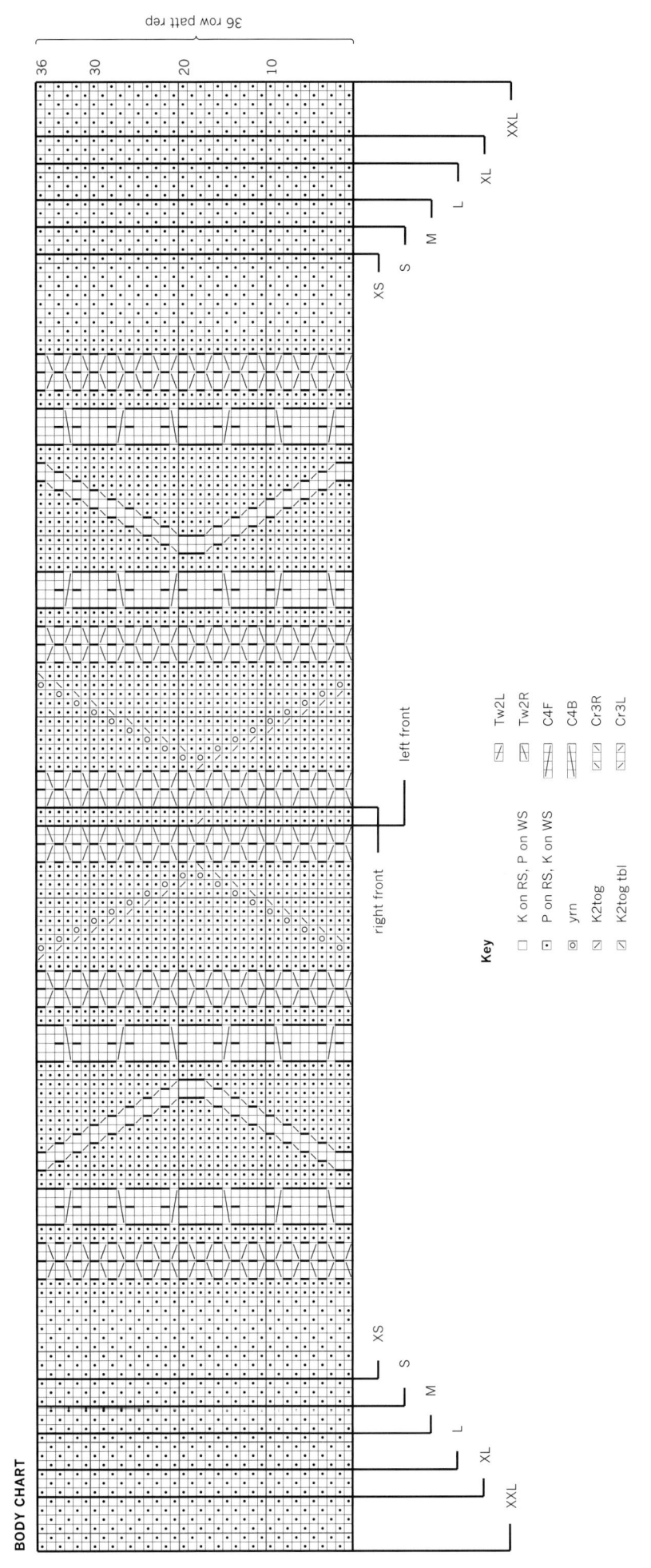

Change to 3¼mm (US 3) needles.
Beg and ending rows as indicated and repeating the 36 row patt repeat throughout, cont in patt from chart for body as follows:
Row 1 (RS): Moss st 7 sts, work rem 63 (66: 69: 73: 76: 82) sts as row 1 of chart.
Row 2: Work first 63 (66: 69: 73: 76: 82) sts as row 2 of chart, moss st 7 sts.
These 2 rows set the sts for rest of right front – front opening edge 7 sts still in moss st with all other sts now in patt.
Complete to match left front, reversing shapings and working first row of neck shaping as follows:
Shape front neck
Next row (RS): Patt 18 (19: 19: 19: 19: 19) sts and slip these sts onto a holder (for neckband), patt to end. 43 (43: 44: 46: 47: 49) sts.

SLEEVES (both alike)
Cast on 61 (63: 65: 69: 71: 73) sts using 2¾mm (US 2) needles.
Row 1 (RS): P1 (0: 1: 1: 0: 1), (P1, K1 tbl) 1 (2: 2: 2: 3: 4) times, (P2, K1 tbl, P1, K1 tbl) 3 times, (P1, K1 tbl) twice, (P2, K1 tbl, P1, K1 tbl) 4 times, P1, (K1 tbl, P1, K1 tbl, P2) 3 times, (K1 tbl, P1) 1 (2: 2: 2: 3: 4) times, P1 (0: 1: 1: 0: 1).
Row 2: K1 (0: 1: 1: 0: 1), (K1, P1) 1 (2: 2: 2: 3: 4) times, (K2, P1, K1, P1) 3 times, (K1, P1) twice, (K2, P1, K1, P1) 4 times, K1, (P1, K1, P1, K2) 3 times, (P1, K1) 1 (2: 2: 2: 3: 4) times, K1 (0: 1: 1: 0: 1).
These 2 rows form rib.

Work in rib for a further 27 rows, ending with a **RS** row.
Row 30 (WS): Rib 6 (7: 8: 10: 11: 12), inc in next st, rib 4, inc in next st, rib 13, inc in next st, rib 3, inc in next st, rib 5, inc in next st, rib 13, inc in next st, rib 4, inc in next st, rib 6 (7: 8: 10: 11: 12).
68 (70: 72: 76: 78: 80) sts.
Change to 3¼mm (US 3) needles.
Beg and ending rows as indicated and repeating the 36 row patt repeat throughout, cont in patt from chart for sleeve as follows:
Work 2 rows, ending with a WS row.
Inc 1 st at each end of next and every foll 12th (12th: 14th: 16th: 14th: 14th) row to 76 (74: 90: 90: 88: 86) sts, then on every foll 14th (14th: 16th: 18th: 16th: 16th) row until there are 88 (90: 92: 94: 98: 100) sts, taking inc sts into moss st.
Cont straight until sleeve measures 45 (46: 47: 48: 49: 50) cm, ending with a WS row.
Shape top
Keeping patt correct, cast off 5 (5: 6: 6: 7: 7) sts at beg of next 2 rows.
78 (80: 80: 82: 84: 86) sts.
Dec 1 st at each end of next 3 rows, then on foll alt row, then on foll 4th row, then on foll 6th row, then on 2 foll 4th rows.
62 (64: 64: 66: 68: 70) sts.
Work 1 row.
Dec 1 st at each end of next and every foll alt row until 56 sts rem, then on foll 7 rows, ending with a WS row.
Cast off rem 42 sts.

MAKING UP
Press all pieces with a warm iron over a damp cloth.
Join both shoulder seams using back stitch or mattress stitch if preferred.
Neckband
With RS facing and using 2¾mm (US 2) needles, slip 18 (19: 19: 19: 19: 19) sts on right front holder onto right needle, rejoin yarn and pick up and knit 27 (27: 27: 30: 30: 30) sts up right side of neck, 41 (43: 43: 45: 45: 45) sts from back, and 27 (27: 27: 30: 30: 30) sts down left side of neck, then patt across 18 (19: 19: 19: 19: 19) sts on left front holder.
131 (135: 135: 143: 143: 143) sts.
Working all sts in moss st as set by front opening edge sts, work 1 row, ending with a WS row.
Next row (RS): K1, P1, K2tog tbl, yfwd (to make 9th buttonhole), moss st to end.
Work in moss st for a further 6 rows, ending with a **RS** row.
Cast off in moss st (on **WS**).
Join side seams. Join sleeve seams. Insert sleeves into armholes. Sew on buttons.

SLEEVE CHART

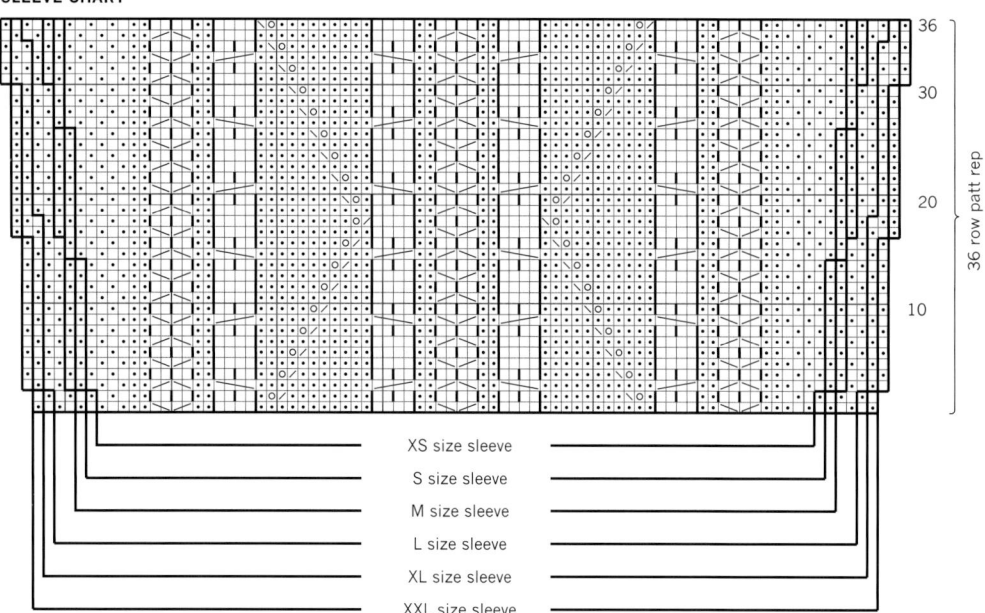

47 (48: 49: 50: 51: 52) cm
18½ (19: 19¼: 19¾: 20: 20½) in

40.5 (43: 45.5: 48: 50.5: 54.5) cm
16 (17: 18: 19: 20: 21½) in

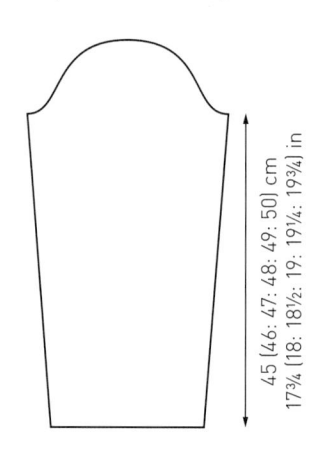

45 (46: 47: 48: 49: 50) cm
17¾ (18: 18½: 19: 19¼: 19¾) in

36 row patt rep

XS size sleeve
S size sleeve
M size sleeve
L size sleeve
XL size sleeve
XXL size sleeve

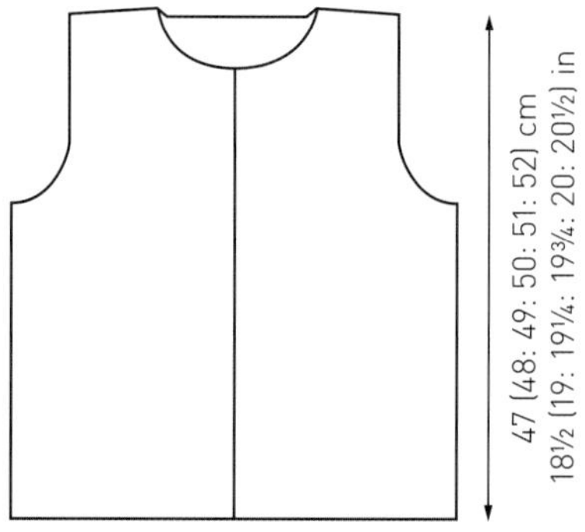

LOVING
Cosy sweater worked in understated garter stitch

Recommendation
Suitable for the knitter with a little experience
Please see pages 26 & 27 for photographs.

	XS	S	M	L	XL	XXL	
To fit bust	81	86	91	97	102	109	cm
	32	34	36	38	40	43	in

Rowan Kidsilk Haze and Fine Lace
Kidsilk Haze
    4   5   5   6   6   7 x 25gm
Fine Lace
    2   3   3   3   3   4 x 50gm
Photographed in Kidsilk Haze in Vanilla with Fine Lace in Porcelaine

Needles
1 pair 3¼mm (no 10) (US 3) needles
1 pair 3¾mm (no 9) (US 5) needles

Tension
21 sts and 40 rows to 10 cm measured over garter stitch using 3¾mm (US 5) needles and one strand each of Kidsilk Haze and Fine Lace held together.
(**Note:** Garter stitch will "drop" a little in wear so it is advisable to stretch the knitting very slightly when measuring your tension.)

Special note: We found it preferable to knit the two yarns together from separate balls rather than winding them together.

BACK
Cast on 86 (92: 98: 102: 108: 116) sts using 3¼mm (US 3) needles and one strand each of Kidsilk Haze and Fine Lace held together. Beg with a RS row, work in g st throughout as follows:
Work 10 rows, ending with a WS row.
Change to 3¾mm (US 5) needles.
Work 36 rows, ending with a WS row.
Place markers at both ends of last row (to denote top of side seam openings).
Next row (RS): K3, K2tog, K to last 5 sts, K2tog tbl, K3.
Working all side seam decreases as set by last row, dec 1 st at each end of 10th and foll 8th row. 80 (86: 92: 96: 102: 110) sts.
Work 19 rows, ending with a WS row.
Next row (RS): K3, M1, K to last 3 sts, M1, K3.
Working all side seam increases as set by last row, inc 1 st at each end of 12th and 3 foll 14th rows.
90 (96: 102: 106: 112: 120) sts.
Cont straight until back measures 38 (38: 39: 39: 39: 39) cm, ending with a WS row.
Shape armholes
Cast off 5 (5: 6: 6: 7: 7) sts at beg of next 2 rows. 80 (86: 90: 94: 98: 106) sts.
Working all armhole decreases in same way as side seam decreases, dec 1 st at each end of next and foll 2 (3: 3: 4: 4: 5) alt rows, then on 1 (2: 3: 3: 4: 5) foll 4th rows.
72 (74: 76: 78: 80: 84) sts.
Cont straight until armhole measures 17.5 (18.5: 18.5: 19.5: 20.5: 21.5) cm, ending with a **RS** row.
Shape back neck
Next row (WS): K20 (20: 21: 21: 22: 24) and slip these sts onto a holder, cast off next 32 (34: 34: 36: 36: 36) sts knitwise, K to end. 20 (20: 21: 21: 22: 24) sts.
Work each side of neck separately.
Next row (RS): K to last 6 sts, K3tog tbl, K3. 18 (18: 19: 19: 20: 22) sts.
Work 1 row.
Shape shoulder
Next row (RS): Cast off 5 (5: 6: 6: 6: 7) sts, K to last 6 sts, K3tog tbl, K3.
Work 1 row.
Cast off 5 (5: 6: 6: 6: 7) sts at beg of next row.
Work 1 row.
Cast off rem 6 (6: 5: 5: 6: 6) sts.
With RS facing, rejoin yarn to sts on holder and K3, K3tog, K to end.
Complete to match first side, reversing shapings.

FRONT
Work as given for back until 27 (27: 27: 31: 31: 31) rows less have been worked than on back to start of shoulder shaping, ending with a **RS** row.
Shape front neck
Next row (WS): K27 (27: 28: 29: 30: 32) and slip these sts onto a holder, cast off next 18 (20: 20: 20: 20: 20) sts knitwise, K to end. 27 (27: 28: 29: 30: 32) sts.
Work each side of neck separately.
Working all neck decreases in same way as back neck and armhole decreases, dec **2** sts at neck edge of next and foll 2 alt rows, then **1** st at neck edge of foll 3 alt rows, then on 1 (1: 1: 2: 2: 2) foll 4th rows, then on foll 6th row. 16 (16: 17: 17: 18: 20) sts.
Work 5 rows, ending with a WS row.
Shape shoulder
Cast off 5 (5: 6: 6: 6: 7) sts at beg of next and foll alt row.
Work 1 row.
Cast off rem 6 (6: 5: 5: 6: 6) sts.
With RS facing, rejoin yarn to sts on holder and K3, K3tog, K to end.
Complete to match first side, reversing shapings.

SLEEVES (both alike)
Cast on 46 (48: 50: 52: 54: 56) sts using 3¼mm (US 3) needles and one strand each of Kidsilk Haze and Fine Lace held together. Beg with a RS row, work in g st throughout as follows:
Work 10 rows, ending with a WS row.
Change to 3¾mm (US 5) needles.
Working all sleeve increases in same way as side seam increases, inc 1 st at each end of 11th and 6 (4: 2: 0: 8: 6) foll 18th rows, then on every foll 20th row until there are 64 (66: 68: 70: 74: 76) sts.
Cont straight until sleeve measures 47 (48: 49: 50: 51: 52) cm, ending with a WS row.

Continued on next page...

ELIN
Classic sweater with V-neck to both back & front

Recommendation
Suitable for the knitter with a little experience
Please see pages 44 & 45 for photographs.

	XS	S	M	L	XL	XXL	
To fit bust	**81**	**86**	**91**	**97**	**102**	**109**	cm
	32	34	36	38	40	43	in

Rowan Alpaca Merino DK
10 10 11 11 12 13 x 25gm
Photographed in Walton

Needles
1 pair 2¾mm (no 12) (US 2) needles
1 pair 3¼mm (no 10) (US 3) needles

Tension
27 sts and 39 rows to 10 cm measured over stocking stitch using 3¼mm (US 3) needles.

BACK and FRONT (both alike)
Cast on 138 (146: 154: 164: 170: 186) sts using 2¾mm (US 2) needles.
Row 1 (RS): P0 (0: 0: 0: 1: 0), K3 (2: 1: 1: 3: 2), *P2, K3, rep from * to last 0 (4: 3: 3: 1: 4) sts, P0 (2: 2: 2: 1: 2), K0 (2: 1: 1: 0: 2).
Row 2: K0 (0: 0: 0: 1: 0), P3 (2: 1: 1: 3: 2), *K2, P3, rep from * to last 0 (4: 3: 3: 1: 4) sts, K0 (2: 2: 2: 1: 2), P0 (2: 1: 1: 0: 2).
These 2 rows form rib.
Work in rib for a further 21 rows, ending with a RS row.
Row 24 (WS): K0 (0: 0: 0: 1: 0), P3 (2: 1: 1: 3: 2), *K2tog, P3, rep from * to last 0 (4: 3: 3: 1: 4) sts, (K2tog) 0 (1: 1: 1: 0: 1) times, K0 (0: 0: 0: 1: 0), P0 (2: 1: 1: 0: 2).
111 (117: 123: 131: 137: 149) sts.
Change to 3¼mm (US 3) needles.
Row 25 (RS): K55 (58: 61: 65: 68: 74), inc in next st, K to end.
112 (118: 124: 132: 138: 150) sts.
Beg with a P row, now work in st st throughout as follows:
Cont straight until work measures 28 (28: 29: 29: 29: 29) cm, ending with a WS row.

Shape raglan armholes
Cast off 5 sts at beg of next 2 rows.
102 (108: 114: 122: 128: 140) sts.
Work 2 (2: 0: 0: 0: 0) rows, ending with a WS row.
Next row (RS): K1, K2tog, K to last 3 sts, K2tog tbl, K1.
Working all raglan armhole decreases as set by last row, cont as follows:
Dec 1 st at each end of 6th (4th: 2nd: 2nd: 2nd: 2nd) and 0 (1: 4: 5: 5: 5) foll 0 (4th: alt: alt: alt: alt) rows.
98 (102: 102: 108: 114: 126) sts.
Work 5 (3: 3: 1: 1: 1) rows, ending with a WS row.

Divide for neck
Next row (RS): K1, K2tog, K43 (45: 45: 48: 51: 57), K2tog tbl, K1 and turn, leaving rem 49 (51: 51: 54: 57: 63) sts on a holder.
Work each side of neck separately.
Next row (WS): (P1, P2tog tbl) 1 (0: 0: 0: 0: 0) times, P to end.
46 (49: 49: 52: 55: 61) sts.
Keeping raglan armhole decreases correct as set and working all neck decreases in same way as raglan armhole decreases, cont as follows:

LOVING – Continued from previous page.

Shape top
Cast off 5 (5: 6: 6: 7: 7) sts at beg of next 2 rows. 54 (56: 56: 58: 60: 62) sts.
Dec 1 st at each end of next and foll alt row, then on foll 4th row, then on 3 foll 6th rows, then on 2 foll 4th rows. 38 (40: 40: 42: 44: 46) sts.
Work 1 row.
Dec 1 st at each end of next and every foll alt row until 32 sts rem, then on foll 5 rows, ending with a WS row.
Cast off rem 22 sts.

MAKING UP
Press all pieces with a warm iron over a damp cloth.
Join both shoulder seams using back stitch or mattress stitch if preferred. Join side seams, leaving side seams open below markers.
Join sleeve seams. Insert sleeves into armholes.

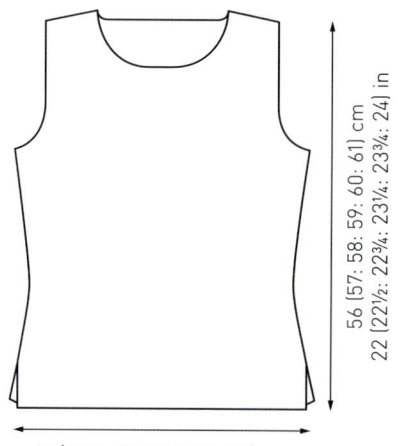

56 [57: 58: 59: 60: 61] cm
22 [22½: 22¾: 23¼: 23¾: 24] in

43 (45.5: 48: 50.5: 53: 57) cm
17 (18: 19: 20: 21: 22½) in

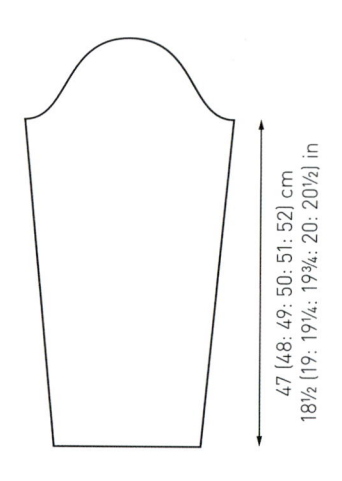

47 (48: 49: 50: 51: 52) cm
18½ (19: 19¼: 19¾: 20: 20½) in

Dec 1 st at raglan armhole edge of 3rd (3rd: 3rd: next: next: next) and foll 0 (0: 0: 1: 5: 15) alt rows, then on 14 (15: 15: 16: 15: 11) foll 4th rows **and at same time** dec 1 st at neck edge of next and foll 28 (30: 30: 30: 28: 26) alt rows, then on 0 (0: 0: 1: 3: 5) foll 4th rows. 2 sts.
Work 1 row, ending with a WS row.
Next row (RS): K2tog and fasten off.
With RS facing, rejoin yarn to rem sts and cont as follows:
Next row (RS): K1, K2tog, K43 (45: 45: 48: 51: 57), K2tog tbl, K1.
Next row (WS): P to last 3 (0: 0: 0: 0: 0) sts, (P2tog, P1) 1 (0: 0: 0: 0: 0) times.
46 (49: 49: 52: 55: 61) sts.
Complete to match first side, reversing shapings.

SLEEVES (both alike)
Cast on 80 (82: 86: 90: 92: 96) sts using 2¾mm (US 2) needles.
Row 1 (RS): P1 (2: 0: 1: 2: 0), K3 (3: 2: 3: 3: 2), *P2, K3, rep from * to last 1 (2: 4: 1: 2: 4) sts, P1 (2: 2: 1: 2: 2), K0 (0: 2: 0: 0: 2).
Row 2: K1 (2: 0: 1: 2: 0), P3 (3: 2: 3: 3: 2), *K2, P3, rep from * to last 1 (2: 4: 1: 2: 4) sts, K1 (2: 2: 1: 2: 2), P0 (0: 2: 0: 0: 2).
These 2 rows form rib.
Work in rib for a further 21 rows, ending with a RS row.
Row 24 (WS): K1 (2: 0: 1: 2: 0), P3 (3: 2: 3: 3: 2), *K2tog, P3, rep from * to last 1 (2: 4: 1: 2: 4) sts, (K2tog) 0 (0: 1: 0: 0: 1) times, K1 (2: 0: 1: 2: 0), P0 (0: 2: 0: 0: 2).
65 (67: 69: 73: 75: 77) sts.
Change to 3¼mm (US 3) needles.
Row 25 (RS): K32 (33: 34: 36: 37: 38), inc in next st, K to end.
66 (68: 70: 74: 76: 78) sts.
Beg with a P row, now work in st st throughout as follows:
Work 1 row, ending with a WS row.
Next row (RS): K3, M1, K to last 3 sts, M1, K3.
Working all sleeve increases as set by last row, inc 1 st at each end of 4th and every foll 4th row to 88 (92: 84: 84: 88: 92) sts, then on every foll 6th row until there are 96 (100: 100: 104: 108: 112) sts.
Cont straight until sleeve measures 28 (29: 30: 31: 32: 33) cm, ending with a WS row.
Shape raglan
Cast off 5 sts at beg of next 2 rows.
86 (90: 90: 94: 98: 102) sts.
Work 2 rows.
Working all raglan decreases in same way as raglan armhole decreases, dec 1 st at each end of next and foll 4th row, then on every foll alt row until 14 sts rem.
Work 1 row, ending with a WS row.
Cast off rem 14 sts.

MAKING UP
Press all pieces with a warm iron over a damp cloth.
Join both front and right back raglan seams using back stitch or mattress stitch if preferred.
Neckband
With RS facing and using 2¾mm (US 2) needles, pick up and knit 12 sts from top of left sleeve, 43 (48: 48: 48: 53: 53) sts down left side of front neck, place marker on needle, pick up and knit 43 (48: 48: 48: 53: 53) sts up right side of front neck, 12 sts from top of right sleeve, and 43 (48: 48: 48: 53: 53) sts down right side of back neck, place second marker on needle, then pick up and knit 43 (48: 48: 48: 53: 53) sts up left side of back neck.
196 (216: 216: 216: 236: 236) sts.
Row 1 (WS): P3, *K2, P3, rep from * to first marker, slip marker onto right needle, **P3, K2, rep from ** to within 3 sts of second marker, P3, slip second marker onto right needle, ***P3, K2, rep from *** to end.
This row sets position of rib.
Keeping rib correct, cont as follows:
Row 2 (RS): *Rib to within 2 sts of marker, K2tog, slip marker onto right needle, K2tog tbl, rep from * once more, rib to end.
Row 3: *Rib to within 2 sts of marker, P2tog tbl, slip marker onto right needle, P2tog, rep from * once more, rib to end.
Rep last 2 rows 3 times more and then row 2 again, ending with a **RS** row.
160 (180: 180: 180: 200: 200) sts.
Cast off in rib (on **WS**), still decreasing either side of markers as before.
Join left back raglan and neckband seam.
Join side and sleeve seams.

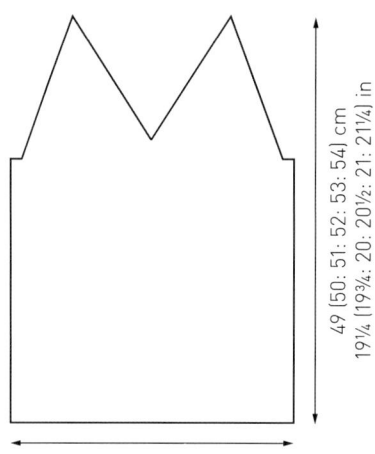

40.5 (43: 45.5: 48: 50.5: 54) cm
16 (17: 18: 19: 20: 21¼) in

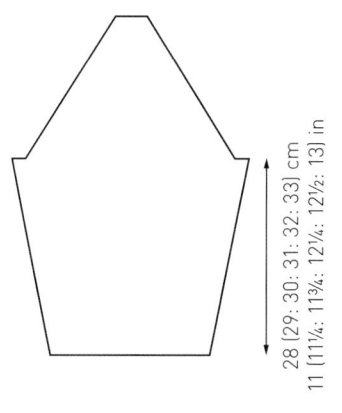

49 (50: 51: 52: 53: 54) cm
19¼ (19¾: 19¾: 20: 20½: 21: 21¼) in

28 (29: 30: 31: 32: 33) cm
11 (11¼: 11¾: 12¼: 12½: 13) in

ESME
Feminine take on the Boyfriend cardigan

Recommendation
Suitable for the knitter with a little experience
Please see pages 32 & 33 for photographs.

	XS	S	M	L	XL	XXL	
To fit bust	**81**	**86**	**91**	**97**	**102**	**109**	cm
	32	34	36	38	40	43	in

Rowan Kidsilk Haze and Fine Lace
Kidsilk Haze
          5   5   6   6   6   7 x 25gm
Fine Lace
          3   3   3   4   4   4 x 50gm
Photographed in Kidsilk Haze in Shadow with Fine Lace in Antique

Needles
1 pair 3¼mm (no 10) (US 3) needles
1 pair 4mm (no 8) (US 6) needles

Buttons – 5

Tension
20 sts and 30 rows to 10 cm measured over stocking stitch using 4mm (US 6) needles and one strand each of Kidsilk Haze and Fine Lace held together.

Special note: We found it preferable to knit the two yarns together from separate balls rather than winding them together.

BACK
Cast on 115 (120: 125: 130: 140: 150) sts using 3¼mm (US 3) needles and one strand each of Kidsilk Haze and Fine Lace held together.
Row 1 (RS): P1, K3, *P2, K3, rep from * to last st, P1.
Row 2: K1, P3, *K2, P3, rep from * to last st, K1.
These 2 rows form rib.
Work in rib for a further 13 rows, ending with a **RS** row.
Row 16 (WS): K1, (P3, K2) 0 (0: 1: 1: 0: 0) times, (P3, K2tog) 22 (23: 22: 23: 27: 29) times, (P3, K2) 0 (0: 1: 1: 0: 0) times, P3, K1. 93 (97: 103: 107: 113: 121) sts.
Change to 4mm (US 6) needles.
Beg with a K row, work in st st throughout as follows:
Cont straight until back measures 47 (47: 48: 48: 48: 48) cm, ending with a WS row.
Shape armholes
Cast off 5 (5: 6: 6: 7: 7) sts at beg of next 2 rows. 83 (87: 91: 95: 99: 107) sts.
Dec 1 st at each end of next 3 (3: 5: 5: 7: 7) rows, then on foll 2 (3: 2: 3: 2: 4) alt rows, then on foll 4th row. 71 (73: 75: 77: 79: 83) sts.
Cont straight until armhole measures 18 (19: 19: 20: 21: 22) cm, ending with a WS row.
Shape shoulders and back neck
Cast off 7 (7: 7: 7: 8: 8) sts at beg of next 2 rows. 57 (59: 61: 63: 63: 67) sts.
Next row (RS): Cast off 7 (7: 7: 7: 8: 8) sts, K until there are 11 (11: 12: 12: 11: 13) sts on right needle and turn, leaving rem sts on a holder.
Work each side of neck separately.
Cast off 4 sts at beg of next row.
Cast off rem 7 (7: 8: 8: 7: 9) sts.
With RS facing, rejoin yarns to rem sts, cast off centre 21 (23: 23: 25: 25: 25) sts, K to end.
Complete to match first side, reversing shapings.

POCKET LININGS (make 2)
Cast on 25 sts using 4mm (US 6) needles and one strand each of Kidsilk Haze and Fine Lace held together.
Beg with a K row, work in st st for 26 rows, ending with a WS row.
Break yarn and leave sts on a holder.

LEFT FRONT
Cast on 61 (66: 66: 71: 76: 81) sts using 3¼mm (US 3) needles and one strand each of Kidsilk Haze and Fine Lace held together.
Row 1 (RS): P1, K3, *P2, K3, rep from * to last 7 sts, K7.
Row 2: K7, P3, *K2, P3, rep from * to last st, K1.
These 2 rows set the sts – front opening edge 7 sts in g st with all other sts in rib.
Cont as set for a further 13 rows, ending with a **RS** row.
Row 16 (WS): K7, (P3, K2) 1 (0: 2: 0: 0: 0) times, (P3, K2tog) 8 (11: 8: 11: 13: 14) times, (P3, K2) 1 (0: 1: 1: 0: 0) times, P3, K1. 53 (55: 58: 60: 63: 67) sts.
Change to 4mm (US 6) needles.
Next row (RS): Knit.
Next row: K7, P to end.
Last 2 rows set the sts for rest of left front – front opening edge 7 sts still in g st with all other sts now in st st.
Keeping sts correct as now set throughout, cont as follows:
Work 24 rows, ending with a WS row.
Place pocket
Next row (RS): K9 (10: 11: 12: 13: 14), slip next 25 sts onto a holder (for pocket top) and, in their place, K across 25 sts of first pocket lining, K to end.
Cont straight until 32 rows less have been worked than on back to start of armhole shaping, ending with a WS row.
Shape front slope
Next row (RS): K to last 10 sts, K2tog tbl, K8.
Working all front slope decreases as set by last row, dec 1 st at front slope edge of 4th and 4 (6: 6: 6: 6: 6) foll 4th rows, then on 1 (0: 0: 0: 0: 0) foll 6th rows. 46 (47: 50: 52: 55: 59) sts.
Work 5 (3: 3: 3: 3: 3) rows, ending with a WS row.
Shape armhole
Cast off 5 (5: 6: 6: 7: 7) sts at beg and dec 1 (0: 0: 1: 1: 0) st at end of next row.
40 (42: 44: 45: 47: 52) sts.
Work 1 row.
Dec 1 st at armhole edge of next 3 (3: 5: 5: 7: 7) rows, then on foll 2 (3: 2: 3: 2: 4) alt rows, then on foll 4th row **and at same time** dec 1 st at front slope edge of 5th (next: next: 3rd: 5th: next) and 1 (2: 2: 2: 1: 3) foll 6th rows.
32 (32: 33: 33: 35: 36) sts.

Dec 1 st at front slope edge **only** on 6th (6th: 6th: 6th: 2nd: 6th) and 3 (3: 3: 3: 4: 3) foll 6th rows. 28 (28: 29: 29: 30: 32) sts.
Cont straight until left front matches back to start of shoulder shaping, ending with a WS row.

Shape shoulder

Cast off 7 (7: 7: 7: 8: 8) sts at beg of next and foll alt row, then 7 (7: 8: 8: 7: 9) sts at beg of foll alt row. 7 sts.
Inc 1 st at end of next row. 8 sts.
Work in g st on these 8 sts only (for back neck border extension) until this strip measures 7 (7.5: 7.5: 8: 8: 8) cm, ending with a WS row.
Cast off.
Mark positions for 5 buttons along left front opening edge – first button to come level with row 5, last button to come 2 cm below start of front slope shaping, and rem 3 buttons evenly spaced between.

RIGHT FRONT

Cast on 61 (66: 66: 71: 76: 81) sts using 3¼mm (US 3) needles and one strand each of Kidsilk Haze and Fine Lace held together.
Row 1 (RS): K10, *P2, K3, rep from * to last st, P1.
Row 2: K1, P3, *K2, P3, rep from * to last 7 sts, K7.
These 2 rows set the sts – front opening edge 7 sts in g st with all other sts in rib.
Cont as set for a further 2 rows, ending with a WS row.
Row 5 (buttonhole row) (RS): K2, K2tog tbl, yfwd (to make a buttonhole), patt to end.
Making a further 4 buttonholes in this way to correspond with positions marked on left front for buttons and noting that no further reference will be made to buttonholes, cont as follows:
Work 10 rows, ending with a **RS** row.
Row 16 (WS): K1, P3, (K2, P3) 1 (0: 1: 1: 0: 0) times, (K2tog, P3) 8 (11: 8: 11: 13: 14) times, (K2, P3) 1 (0: 2: 0: 0: 0) times, K7. 53 (55: 58: 60: 63: 67) sts.
Change to 4mm (US 6) needles.
Next row (RS): Knit.
Next row: P to last 7 sts, K7.
Last 2 rows set the sts for rest of right front – front opening edge 7 sts still in g st with all other sts now in st st.
Keeping sts correct as now set throughout, cont as follows:
Work 24 rows, ending with a WS row.

Place pocket

Next row (RS): K19 (20: 22: 23: 25: 28), slip next 25 sts onto a holder (for pocket top) and, in their place, K across 25 sts of second pocket lining, K to end.
Cont straight until 32 rows less have been worked than on back to start of armhole shaping, ending with a WS row.

Shape front slope

Next row (RS): K8, K2tog, K to end.
Working all front slope decreases as set by last row, complete to match left front, reversing shapings.

SLEEVES (both alike)

Cast on 54 (56: 58: 60: 64: 66) sts using 3¼mm (US 3) needles and one strand each of Kidsilk Haze and Fine Lace held together.
Row 1 (RS): P0 (0: 0: 1: 0: 0), K1 (2: 3: 3: 1: 2), *P2, K3, rep from * to last 3 (4: 0: 1: 3: 4) sts, P2 (2: 0: 1: 2: 2), K1 (2: 0: 0: 1: 2).
Row 2: K0 (0: 0: 1: 0: 0), P1 (2: 3: 3: 1: 2), *K2, P3, rep from * to last 3 (4: 0: 1: 3: 4) sts, K2 (2: 0: 1: 2: 2), P1 (2: 0: 0: 1: 2).
These 2 rows form rib.
Work in rib for a further 15 rows, ending with a **RS** row.
Row 18 (WS): K0 (0: 0: 1: 0: 0), P1 (2: 3: 3: 1: 2), *K2tog, P3, rep from * to last 3 (4: 0: 1: 3: 4) sts, (K2tog) 1 (1: 0: 0: 1: 1) times, K0 (0: 0: 1: 0: 0), P1 (2: 0: 0: 1: 2). 43 (45: 47: 49: 51: 53) sts.
Change to 4mm (US 6) needles.
Beg with a K row, work in st st throughout as follows:
Work 2 rows, ending with a WS row.
Next row (RS): K3, M1, K to last 3 sts, M1, K3.
Working all sleeve increases as set by last row, inc 1 st at each end of 12th (12th: 14th: 14th: 12th: 12th) and every foll 12th (14th: 14th: 14th: 12th: 12th) row to 51 (63: 65: 63: 61: 59) sts, then on every foll 14th (-: -: 16th: 14th: 14th) row until there are 61 (-: -: 67: 71: 73) sts.
Cont straight until sleeve measures 47 (48: 49: 50: 51: 52) cm, ending with a WS row.

Shape top

Cast off 5 (5: 6: 6: 7: 7) sts at beg of next 2 rows. 51 (53: 53: 55: 57: 59) sts.
Dec 1 st at each end of next and foll 2 alt rows, then on foll 4th row, then on foll 6th row, then on 2 foll 4th rows. 37 (39: 39: 41: 43: 45) sts.
Work 1 row.
Dec 1 st at each end of next and every foll alt row until 31 sts rem, then on foll 3 rows, ending with a WS row.
Cast off rem 25 sts.

MAKING UP

Press all pieces with a warm iron over a damp cloth.
Join both shoulder seams using back stitch or mattress stitch if preferred. Join ends of back neck border extensions, then sew one edge to back neck.

Pocket tops (both alike)

Slip 25 sts on pocket holder onto 3¼mm (US 3) needles and rejoin one strand each of Kidsilk Haze and Fine Lace held together with **WS** facing.
Row 1 (WS): (K1, M1, P3) 6 times, M1, K1. 32 sts.
Row 2: P2, *K3, P2, rep from * to end.
Row 3: K2, *P3, K2, rep from * to end.
Last 2 rows form rib.
Work in rib for a further 7 rows, ending with a **RS** row.
Cast off in rib (on **WS**).
Sew pocket linings in place on inside, then neatly sew down ends of pocket tops.
Join side seams. Join sleeve seams.
Insert sleeves into armholes.
Sew on buttons.

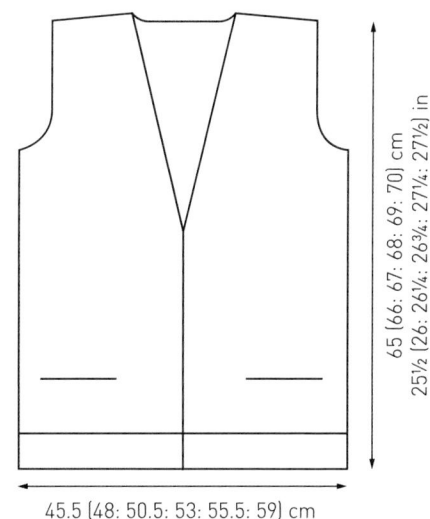

45.5 (48: 50.5: 53: 55.5: 59) cm
18 (19: 20: 21: 22: 23¼) in

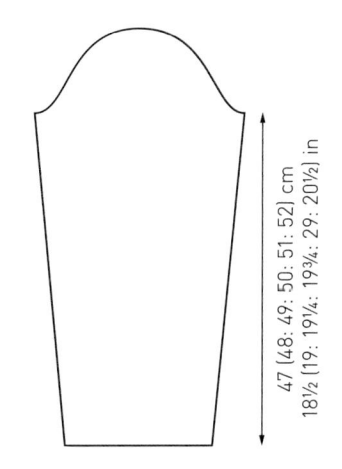

65 (66: 67: 68: 69: 70) cm
25½ (26: 26¼: 26¾: 27¼: 27½) in

47 (48: 49: 50: 51: 52) cm
18½ (19: 19¼: 19¾: 29: 20½) in

GIFT
Neat sweater worked in pretty eyelets

Recommendation
Suitable for the more experienced knitter
Please see pages 30 & 31 for photographs.

	XS	S	M	L	XL	XXL	
To fit bust	**81**	**86**	**91**	**97**	**102**	**109**	cm
	32	34	36	38	40	43	in

Rowan Kidsilk Haze
3 3 4 4 4 5 x 25gm
Photographed in Majestic

Needles
1 pair 2¾mm (no 12) (US 2) needles
1 pair 3¼mm (no 10) (US 3) needles
Cable needle

Tension
25 sts and 34 rows to 10 cm measured over stocking stitch using 3¼mm (US 3) needles.

Special abbreviations
C4B = slip next 2 sts onto cable needle and leave at back of work, K2, then K2 from cable needle; **C4F** = slip next 2 sts onto cable needle and leave at front of work, K2, then K2 from cable needle.

BACK
Cast on 195 (207: 219: 231: 243: 267) sts using 2¾mm (US 2) needles and yarn DOUBLE.
Break off one strand of yarn and cont using SINGLE strand of yarn throughout as follows:
Row 1 (RS): K3, *cast off next 3 sts, K2 (3 sts on right needle after cast-off), rep from * to end. 99 (105: 111: 117: 123: 135) sts.
Dec 0 (0: 0: 0: 0: 1) st at each end of next row, work in g st for 10 rows, ending with a **RS** row.
Row 12 (WS): K17 (20: 23: 26: 29: 34), inc in next st, K62, inc in next st, K18 (21: 24: 27: 30: 35).
101 (107: 113: 119: 125: 135) sts.
Change to 3¼mm (US 3) needles.
Beg and ending rows as indicated and repeating the 12 and 16 row patt repeats throughout, cont in patt from chart as follows:
Cont straight until back measures 30 (30: 31: 31: 31: 31) cm, ending with a WS row.
Shape armholes
Keeping patt correct, cast off 5 (5: 6: 6: 7: 7) sts at beg of next 2 rows.
91 (97: 101: 107: 111: 121) sts.
Dec 1 st at each end of next 1 (3: 3: 5: 5: 7) rows, then on foll 2 (2: 3: 2: 3: 4) alt rows.
85 (87: 89: 93: 95: 99) sts.
Cont straight until armhole measures 17 (18: 18: 19: 20: 21) cm, ending with a WS row.
Shape shoulders and back neck
Cast off 6 (6: 7: 7: 7: 8) sts at beg of 2 rows. 73 (75: 75: 79: 81: 83) sts.
Next row (RS): Cast off 6 (6: 7: 7: 7: 8) sts, patt until there are 11 (11: 10: 11: 12: 12) sts on right needle and turn, leaving rem sts on a holder.
Work each side of neck separately.
Cast off 4 sts at beg of next row.
Cast off rem 7 (7: 6: 7: 8: 8) sts.
With RS facing, rejoin yarn to rem sts, cast off centre 39 (41: 41: 43: 43: 43) sts, patt to end.
Complete to match first side, reversing shapings.

FRONT
Work as given for back until 32 (32: 32: 34: 34: 34) rows less have been worked than on back to start of shoulder shaping, ending with a WS row.

Shape front neck
Next row (RS): Patt 31 (31: 32: 34: 35: 37) sts and turn, leaving rem sts on a holder.
Work each side of neck separately.
Keeping patt correct, dec 1 st at neck edge of next 6 rows, then on foll 4 (4: 4: 5: 5: 5) alt rows, then on foll 4th row, then on foll 6th row.
19 (19: 20: 21: 22: 24) sts.
Work 7 rows, ending with a WS row.
Shape shoulder
Cast off 6 (6: 7: 7: 7: 8) sts at beg of next and foll alt row.
Work 1 row.
Cast off rem 7 (7: 6: 7: 8: 8) sts.
With RS facing, rejoin yarn to rem sts, cast off centre 23 (25: 25: 25: 25: 25) sts, patt to end.
Complete to match first side, reversing shapings.

SLEEVES (both alike)
Cast on 123 (129: 135: 135: 147: 147) sts using 2¾mm (US 2) needles and yarn DOUBLE.
Break off one strand of yarn and cont using SINGLE strand of yarn throughout as follows:
Row 1 (RS): K3, *cast off next 3 sts, K2 (3 sts on right needle after cast-off), rep from * to end. 63 (66: 69: 69: 75: 75) sts.
Inc 2 (1: 0: 2: 0: 2) sts evenly across next row, work in g st for 5 rows, ending with a WS row.
65 (67: 69: 71: 75: 77) sts.
Change to 3¼mm (US 3) needles.
Next row (RS): K3, M1, K to last 3 sts, M1, K3.
Beg with a P row and working all sleeve increases as set by last row, cont in st st, shaping sides by inc 1 st at each end of 8th and foll 8th row.
71 (73: 75: 77: 81: 83) sts.
Work 5 rows, ending with a WS row.
Shape top
Cast off 5 (5: 6: 6: 7: 7) sts at beg of next 2 rows. 61 (63: 63: 65: 67: 69) sts.
Dec 1 st at each end of next and foll alt row, then on 5 foll 4th rows.
47 (49: 49: 51: 53: 55) sts.
Work 1 row.
Dec 1 st at each end of next and every foll alt row until 43 sts rem, then on foll 7 rows, ending with a WS row.
Cast off rem 29 sts.

MAKING UP
Press all pieces with a warm iron over a damp cloth.
Join right shoulder seam using back stitch or mattress stitch if preferred.

Neckband
With RS facing and using 2¾mm (US 2) needles, pick up and knit 23 (24: 24: 26: 26: 26) sts down left side of front neck, 23 (25: 25: 25: 25: 25) sts from front, 23 (24: 24: 26: 26: 26) sts up right side of front neck, and 48 (50: 50: 52: 52: 52) sts from back.
117 (123: 123: 129: 129: 129) sts.
Work in g st for 5 rows, ending with a WS row.
Row 6 (RS): K3, *turn and cast on 3 sts, turn and K3, rep from * to end.
Join in second strand of yarn.
Using yarn DOUBLE cast off all sts knitwise (on **WS**).
Join left shoulder and neckband seam.
Lay garment flat and carefully press shoulder and neck area so that neckband lays flat.
Join side seams. Join sleeve seams. Insert sleeves into armholes.

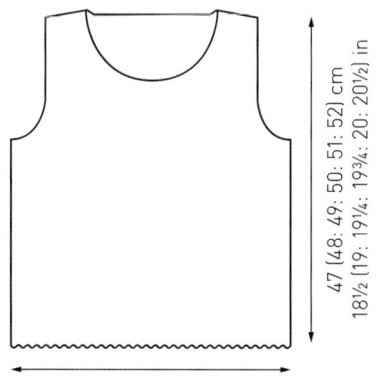

47 (48: 49: 50: 51: 52) cm
18½ (19: 19¾: 19¾: 20: 20½) in

39.5 (42: 44.5: 47: 49.5: 53.5) cm
15½ (16½: 17½: 18½: 19½: 21) in

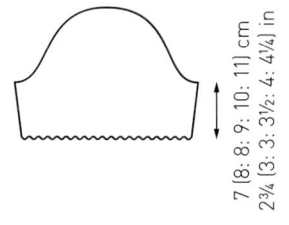

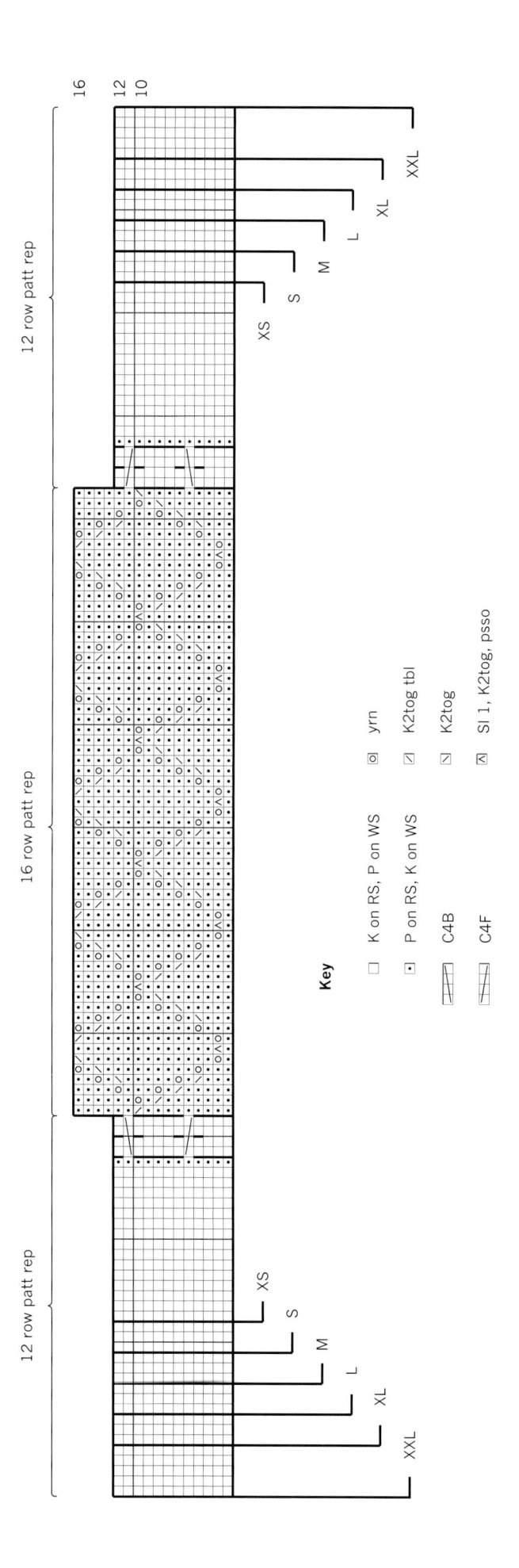

7 (8: 8: 9: 10: 11) cm
2¾ (3: 3: 3½: 4: 4¼) in

Key
☐ K on RS, P on WS
▪ P on RS, K on WS
C4B
C4F
○ yrn
╲ K2tog tbl
╱ K2tog
▲ Sl 1, K2tog, psso

SCAPE
Generous raglan sweater worked in soft ribbing

Recommendation
Suitable for the knitter with a little experience
Please see pages 37, 38 & 39 for photographs.

	XS	S	M	L	XL	XXL	
To fit bust	81	86	91	97	102	109	cm
	32	34	36	38	40	43	in

Rowan Kid Classic and Kidsilk Haze
Kid Classic
        7   8   8   9   9   10 x 50gm
Kidsilk Haze
        5   6   6   7   7   8 x 25gm
Photographed in Kid Classic in Cement with Kidsilk Haze in Majestic

Needles
1 pair 4mm (no 8) (US 6) needles
1 pair 4½mm (no 7) (US 7) needles
1 pair 5mm (no 6) (US 8) needles

Tension
21 sts and 28 rows to 10 cm measured over pattern using 5mm (US 8) needles and one strand each of Kid Classic and Kidsilk Haze held together.

Special note: We found it preferable to knit the two yarns together from separate balls rather than winding them together.

BACK
Cast on 103 (107: 113: 117: 123: 131) sts using 4½mm (US 7) needles and one strand each of Kid Classic and Kidsilk Haze held together.
Row 1 (RS): P0 (0: 1: 1: 0: 0), (K1, P1) 2 (2: 2: 2: 3: 3) times, *K1, P1, K2, rep from * to last 7 (7: 8: 8: 9: 9) sts, K1, (P1, K1) 3 (3: 3: 3: 4: 4) times, P0 (0: 1: 1: 0: 0).
Row 2: P0 (0: 1: 1: 0: 0), (K1, P1) 2 (2: 2: 2: 3: 3) times, *K3, P1, rep from * to last 7 (7: 8: 8: 9: 9) sts, K3, (P1, K1) 2 (2: 2: 2: 3: 3) times, P0 (0: 1: 1: 0: 0).
These 2 rows set the sts – 4 (4: 5: 5: 6: 6) sts in moss st at each end of row and all other sts in patt.
Cont as set for a further 8 rows, ending with a WS row.
Change to 5mm (US 8) needles.
Work a further 30 (30: 32: 32: 34: 34) rows, ending with a WS row.
Place markers at both ends of last row (to denote top of side seam openings).
Now working **all** sts in patt, cont as follows:
Cont straight until back measures 34 (34: 34.5: 35: 35: 35) cm, ending with a WS row.
Shape raglan armholes
Keeping patt correct, cast off 5 (5: 6: 6: 7: 7) sts at beg of next 2 rows.
93 (97: 101: 105: 109: 117) sts.
Work 2 rows, ending with a WS row.
Next row (RS): (P1, K3) twice, P2tog, patt to last 10 sts, P2tog tbl, (K3, P1) twice.
Next row: K2, P1, K3, P1, K2, patt to last 9 sts, K2, P1, K3, P1, K2.
Next row: (P1, K3) twice, (P2tog) 1 (0: 1: 0: 1: 1) times, P0 (1: 0: 1: 0: 0), patt to last 10 (9: 10: 9: 10: 10) sts, (P2tog tbl) 1 (0: 1: 0: 1: 1) times, P0 (1: 0: 1: 0: 0), (K3, P1) twice.
89 (95: 97: 103: 105: 113) sts.
Next row: K2, P1, K3, P1, K2, patt to last 9 sts, K2, P1, K3, P1, K2.
Working all raglan armhole decreases and raglan armhole sts correct as set by last 4 rows, cont as follows:
Dec 1 st at each end of next and 0 (1: 0: 0: 0: 0) foll 4th row, then on foll 19 (19: 21: 22: 23: 25) alt rows. 49 (53: 53: 57: 57: 61) sts.
Work 1 row, ending with a WS row.
Cast off in patt.

FRONT
Work as given for back until 61 (65: 65: 69: 69: 73) sts rem in raglan armhole shaping.
Work 1 row, ending with a WS row.
Shape front neck
Next row (RS): (P1, K3) twice, P2tog, patt 8 sts and turn, leaving rem sts on a holder. 17 sts.
Work each side of neck separately.
Keeping patt and raglan armhole decreases correct as set, cast off 4 sts at beg (neckedge) of next and foll 2 alt rows
and at same time dec 1 st at raglan armhole edge of 2nd row. 4 sts.
Work 1 row.
Cast off rem 4 sts.
With RS facing, rejoin yarn to rem sts, cast off centre 25 (29: 29: 33: 33: 37) sts, patt to last 10 sts, P2tog tbl, (K3, P1) twice. 17 sts.
Complete to match first side, reversing shapings.

SLEEVES (both alike)
Cast on 59 (63: 65: 69: 71: 71) sts using 4½mm (US 7) needles and one strand each of Kid Classic and Kidsilk Haze held together.
Row 1 (RS): K1 (1: 2: 2: 3: 3), *P1, K3, rep from * to last 2 (2: 3: 3: 4: 4) sts, P1, K1 (1: 2: 2: 3: 3).
Row 2: K0 (0: 0: 0: 1: 1), P0 (0: 1: 1: 1: 1), K1, *K2, P1, K1, rep from * to last 2 (2: 3: 3: 0: 0) sts, K2 (2: 2: 2: 0: 0), P0 (0: 1: 1: 0: 0).
These 2 rows form patt.
Cont in patt for a further 8 rows, ending with a WS row.
Change to 5mm (US 8) needles.
Work 6 rows, ending with a WS row.
Next row (RS): Patt 6 (6: 7: 7: 8: 8) sts, M1, patt to last 6 (6: 7: 7: 8: 8) sts, M1, patt 6 (6: 7: 7: 8: 8) sts.
Working all sleeve increases as set by last row (and keeping edge 6 (6: 7: 7: 8: 8) sts correct in patt as set), inc 1 st at each end of 10th and 4 (4: 4: 5: 6: 6) foll 10th rows, then on 2 (2: 2: 1: 0: 0) foll 8th rows, taking sts between increases into patt. 75 (79: 81: 85: 87: 87) sts.
Cont straight until sleeve measures 34 (34: 34.5: 35: 35: 35) cm, ending with a WS row.

Shape raglan
Keeping patt correct, cast off 5 (5: 6: 6: 7: 7) sts at beg of next 2 rows.
65 (69: 69: 73: 73: 73) sts.
Work 2 rows, ending with a WS row.
Working all raglan decreases in same way as raglan armhole decreases, dec 1 st at each end of next and 1 (1: 1: 2: 4: 5) foll 4th rows, then on foll 17 (19: 19: 18: 16: 15) alt rows, ending with a **RS** row.
27 (27: 27: 31: 31: 31) sts.

Left sleeve only
Cast off 9 sts at beg of next row, then dec 1 st at beg of foll row.
17 (17: 17: 21: 21: 21) sts.
Cast off 8 (8: 8: 10: 10: 10) sts at beg of next row, then dec 1 st at **end** of foll row, ending with a **RS** row.

Right sleeve only
Work 1 row, ending with a WS row.
Cast off 9 sts at beg and dec 1 st at end of next row.
17 (17: 17: 21: 21: 21) sts.
Work 1 row.
Cast off 9 (9: 9: 11: 11: 11) sts at beg of next row.
Work 1 row, ending with a WS row.

Both sleeves
Cast off rem 8 (8: 8: 10: 10: 10) sts.

MAKING UP
Press all pieces with a warm iron over a damp cloth.
Join both front and right back raglan seams using back stitch or mattress stitch if preferred.

Neckband
With RS facing, using 4mm (US 6) needles and one strand each of Kid Classic and Kidsilk Haze held together, pick up and knit 24 (24: 24: 28: 28: 28) sts from top of left sleeve, 1 st at top of raglan seam, 13 sts down left side of front neck, 25 (29: 29: 33: 33: 37) sts from front,
13 sts up right side of front neck, 1 st at top of raglan seam, 23 (23: 23: 27: 27: 27) sts from top of right sleeve, 1 st at top of raglan seam, then 48 (52: 52: 56: 56: 60) sts from back.
149 (157: 157: 173: 173: 181) sts.
Row 1 (WS): P1, *K1, P1, rep from * to end.
Row 2: K1, *P1, K1 tbl, rep from * to last 2 sts, P1, K1.
These 2 rows form rib.
Cont in rib for a further 8 rows, ending with a **RS** row.
Cast off in rib (on **WS**).
Join left back raglan and neckband seam.
Join side and sleeve seams, leaving side seams open below markers.

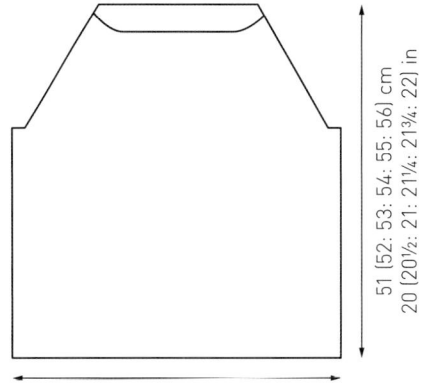

49 (51: 54: 56: 58.5: 62.5) cm
19¼ (20¼: 21¼: 22: 23: 24½) in

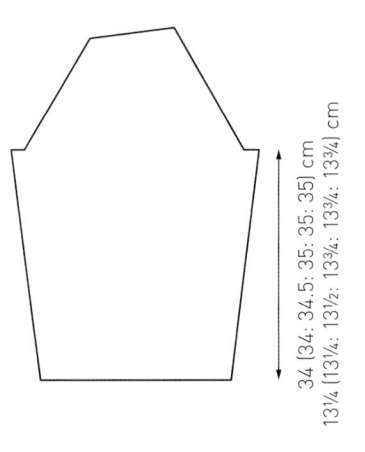

51 (52: 53: 54: 55: 56) cm
20 (20½: 21: 21¼: 21¾: 22) in

34 (34: 34.5: 35: 35: 35) cm
13¼ (13¼: 13½: 13¾: 13¾: 13¾) cm

PITCH
Longline sleeveless cardigan with belt & side vents

Recommendation
Suitable for the novice knitter
Please see pages 40 & 41 for photographs.

	XS	S	M	L	XL	XXL	
To fit bust	81	86	91	97	102	109	cm
	32	34	36	38	40	43	in

Rowan Brushed Fleece
   6   7   8   8   9   9 x 50gm
Photographed in Peat

Needles
1 pair 5mm (no 6) (US 8) needles
1 pair 6mm (no 4) (US 10) needles

Tension
14 sts and 21 rows to 10 cm measured over stocking stitch using 6mm (US 10) needles.

BACK
Cast on 78 (83: 88: 93: 98: 103) sts using 5mm (US 8) needles.
Row 1 (RS): (K1, P1) twice, K4, *P2, K3, rep from * to last 5 sts, K1, (P1, K1) twice.
Row 2: (K1, P1) twice, K1, P3, *K2, P3, rep from * to last 5 sts, (K1, P1) twice, K1.
These 2 rows set the sts – 5 sts in moss st at each end of rows with all other sts in rib.
Cont as set for a further 11 rows, ending with a **RS** row.
Row 14 (WS): Moss st 5 sts, P3, (K2tog, P3) to last 5 sts, moss st 5 sts.
65 (69: 73: 77: 81: 85) sts.
Change to 6mm (US 10) needles.
Row 15 (RS): Moss st 5 sts, K to last 5 sts, moss st 5 sts.
Row 16: Moss st 5 sts, P to last 5 sts, moss st 5 sts.
Last 2 rows set the sts – 5 sts still in moss st at each end of rows with all other sts now in st st.
Cont as now set until back measures 29 (29: 30: 30: 30: 30) cm, ending with a WS row.
Place markers at both ends of last row (to denote top of side seam openings).
Now working all sts in st st, beg with a K row, cont as follows:
Work 18 rows, ending with a WS row.
Next row (RS): K3, K2tog, K to last 5 sts, K2tog tbl, K3.
Working all side seam decreases as set by last row, dec 1 st at each end of 6th and 2 foll 6th rows, then on 2 foll 4th rows.
53 (57: 61: 65: 69: 73) sts.
Work 13 rows, ending with a WS row.
Next row (RS): K3, M1, K to last 3 sts, M1, K3.
Working all side seam increases as set by last row, inc 1 st at each end of 6th and foll 6th row.
59 (63: 67: 71: 75: 79) sts.
Work 5 rows, ending with a WS row.
(Back measures approx.
65 (65: 66: 66: 66: 66) cm).
Shape armholes
Cast off 2 (2: 2: 3: 3: 3) sts at beg of next 2 rows. 55 (59: 63: 65: 69: 73) sts.
Next row (RS): K2, K2tog, K to last 4 sts, K2tog tbl, K2.
Working all armhole decreases as set by last row, dec 1 st at each end of next and foll 6 (7: 8: 9: 10: 11) alt rows, then on foll 4th row. 37 (39: 41: 41: 43: 45) sts.
Cont straight until armhole measures 25 (26: 26: 27: 28: 29) cm, ending with a WS row.
Shape shoulders and back neck
Next row (RS): Cast off 5 (5: 5: 5: 5: 6) sts, K until there are 9 (9: 10: 9: 10: 10) sts on right needle and turn, leaving rem sts on a holder.
Work each side of neck separately.
Cast off 4 sts at beg of next row.
Cast off rem 5 (5: 6: 5: 6: 6) sts.
With RS facing, rejoin yarn to rem sts, cast off centre 9 (11: 11: 13: 13: 13) sts, K to end.
Complete to match first side, reversing shapings.

LEFT FRONT
Cast on 38 (43: 43: 48: 48: 53) sts using 5mm (US 8) needles.
Row 1 (RS): (K1, P1) twice, K4, *P2, K3, rep from * to last 5 sts, K1, (P1, K1) twice.
Row 2: (K1, P1) twice, K1, P3, *K2, P3, rep from * to last 5 sts, (K1, P1) twice, K1.
These 2 rows set the sts – 5 sts in moss st at each end of rows with all other sts in rib.
Cont as set for a further 11 rows, ending with a **RS** row.
Row 14 (WS): Moss st 5 sts, P3, (K2, P3) 1 (0: 1: 0: 1: 0) times, (K2tog, P3) 3 (6: 4: 7: 5: 8) times, (K2, P3) 1 (0: 1: 0: 1: 0) times, moss st 5 sts. 35 (37: 39: 41: 43: 45) sts.
Change to 6mm (US 10) needles.
Row 15 (RS): Moss st 5 sts, K to last 5 sts, moss st 5 sts.
Row 16: Moss st 5 sts, P to last 5 sts, moss st 5 sts.
Last 2 rows set the sts – 5 sts still in moss st at each end of rows with all other sts now in st st.
Cont as now set until left front measures 29 (29: 30: 30: 30: 30) cm, ending with a WS row.**
Place marker at end of last row (to denote top of side seam opening).
Next row (RS): K to last 5 sts, moss st 5 sts.
Next row: Moss st 5 sts, P to end.
Last 2 rows set the sts for rest of left front – 5 sts still in moss st at front opening edge with all other sts now in st st.

Keeping sts correct as now set, cont as follows:
Work 16 rows, ending with a WS row.
Working all side seam decreases as set by back, dec 1 st at beg of next and 3 foll 6th rows, then on 2 foll 4th rows.
29 (31: 33: 35: 37: 39) sts.
Work 13 rows, ending with a WS row.
Working all side seam increases as set by back, inc 1 st at beg of next row.
30 (32: 34: 36: 38: 40) sts.
Work 1 row, ending with a WS row.
Shape front slope
Next row (RS): K to last 7 sts, K2tog tbl, moss st 5 sts.
29 (31: 33: 35: 37: 39) sts.
Working all front slope decreases as set by last row, cont as follows:
Inc 1 st at side seam edge of 4th and foll 6th row **and at same time** dec 1 st at front slope edge of 10th (10th: 10th: 8th: 8th: 8th) row.
30 (32: 34: 36: 38: 40) sts.
Work 5 rows, ending with a WS row.
Shape armhole
Cast off 2 (2: 2: 3: 3: 3) sts at beg and dec 0 (0: 0: 1: 1: 1) st at end of next row.
28 (30: 32: 32: 34: 36) sts.
Work 1 row.
Working all armhole decreases as set by back, dec 1 st at armhole edge of next and foll 7 (8: 9: 10: 11: 12) alt rows, then on foll 4th row **and at same time** dec 1 st at front slope edge on 5th (3rd: 3rd: 7th: 7th: 9th) and 1 (1: 2: 1: 2: 2) foll 12th (10th: 10th: 8th: 10th: 10th) rows, then on foll – (-: -: 10th: -: -) row.
17 (18: 18: 17: 18: 19) sts.
Dec 1 st at front slope edge **only** on 10th (2nd: 10th: 10th: 10th: 10th) and 1 (2: 1: 1: 1: 1) foll 12th (10th: 10th: 10th: 10th: 10th) rows.
15 (15: 16: 15: 16: 17) sts.
Cont straight until left front matches back to start of shoulder shaping, ending with a WS row.
Shape shoulder
Cast off 5 (5: 5: 5: 5: 6) sts at beg of next row, then 5 (5: 6: 5: 6: 6) sts at beg of foll alt row. 5 sts.
Inc 1 st at end of next row. 6 sts.
Work in moss st on these 6 sts only (for back neck border extension) until this strip measures 6 (6.5: 6.5: 7.5: 7.5: 7.5) cm, ending with a WS row.
Cast off.

RIGHT FRONT
Work as given for left front to **.
Place marker at beg of last row (to denote top of side seam opening).

Next row (RS): Moss st 5 sts, K to end.
Next row: P to last 5 sts, moss st 5 sts.
Last 2 rows set the sts for rest of right front – 5 sts still in moss st at front opening edge with all other sts now in st st.
Keeping sts correct as now set, cont as follows:
Work 16 rows, ending with a WS row.
Working all side seam decreases as set by back, dec 1 st at end of next and 3 foll 6th rows, then on 2 foll 4th rows.
29 (31: 33: 35: 37: 39) sts.
Work 13 rows, ending with a WS row.
Working all side seam increases as set by back, inc 1 st at end of next row.
30 (32: 34: 36: 38: 40) sts.
Work 1 row, ending with a WS row.
Shape front slope
Next row (RS): Moss st 5 sts, K2tog, K to end.
29 (31: 33: 35: 37: 39) sts.
Working all front slope decreases as set by last row, complete to match left front, reversing shapings.

MAKING UP
Press all pieces with a warm iron over a damp cloth.
Join both shoulder seams using back stitch or mattress stitch if preferred. Join ends of back neck border extensions, then sew one edge to back neck.
Armhole borders (both alike)
With RS facing and using 5mm (US 8) needles, pick up and knit 83 (83: 83: 88: 88: 93) sts all round armhole.
Row 1 (WS): P3, *K2, P3, rep from * to end.
Row 2: K3, *P2, K3, rep from * to end.
Last 2 rows form rib.
Cont in rib for a further 4 rows, ending with a **RS** row.
Cast off in rib (on **WS**).
Belt
Cast on 7 sts using 5mm (US 8) needles.
Row 1 (RS): K1, *P1, K1, rep from * to end.
Row 2: As row 1.
These 2 rows form moss st.
Cont in moss st until belt measures 165 (170: 175: 180: 185: 190) cm, ending with a WS row.
Cast off.
Join side seams **only**, leaving seams open below markers – do NOT join armhole border seams. Using photograph as a guide, overlap ends of armhole borders and neatly sew row-end edges of borders to armhole pick-up rows.

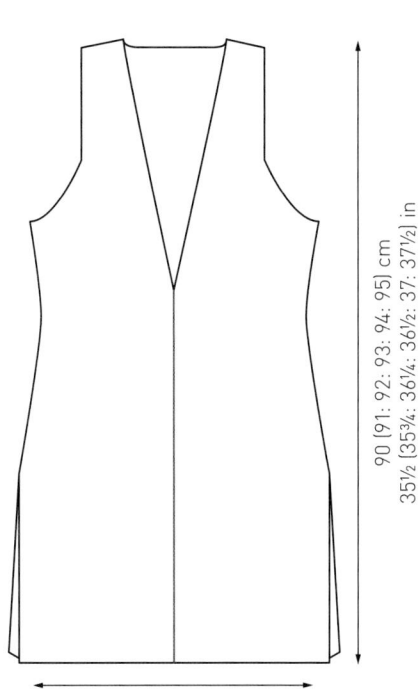

41.5 (44: 46.5: 49: 51.5: 55) cm
16¼ (17¼: 18¼: 19¼: 20½: 21¾) in

45.5 (48: 50.5: 53: 55.5: 59.5) cm
18 (19: 20: 21: 22: 23½) in

90 (91: 92: 93: 94: 95) cm
35½ (35¾: 36¼: 36½: 37: 37½) in

FELL
Fitted cardigan worked in aran braids

Recommendation
Suitable for the knitter with a little experience
Please see pages 50 & 51 for photographs.

	XS	S	M	L	XL	XXL	
To fit bust	81	86	91	97	102	109	cm
	32	34	36	38	40	43	in

Rowan Big Wool

| | 7 | 7 | 8 | 8 | 9 | 10 | x100gm |

Photographed in Smoky

Needles
1 pair 8mm (no 0) (US 11) needles
1 pair 9mm (no 00) (US 13) needles

Buttons – 7

Tension
10 sts and 14 rows to 10 cm measured over stocking stitch using 9mm (US 13) needles.

Special abbreviations
Tw2L = K into back of second st on left needle, then K first st and slip both sts off left needle together; **Tw2R** = K into front of second st on left needle, then K first st and slip both sts off left needle together.

Pattern note: When casting off across top of the braids (worked as Tw2L and Tw2R), dec 2 sts to ensure the edge does not stretch too much. These decreased sts are NOT included in any st counts.

BACK
Cast on 41 (43: 45: 49: 51: 55) sts using 8mm (US 11) needles.
Row 1 (RS): K0 (1: 0: 0: 1: 1), *P1, K1, rep from * to last 1 (0: 1: 1: 0: 0) st, P1 (0: 1: 1: 0: 0).
Row 2: As row 1.
These 2 rows form moss st.
Work in moss st for a further 3 rows, ending with a **RS** row.
Row 6 (WS): Moss st 7 (8: 9: 11: 12: 14) sts, inc in next st, moss st 8 sts, inc in next st, (moss st 3 sts, inc in next st) twice, moss st 8 sts, inc in next st, moss st 7 (8: 9: 11: 12: 14) sts. 46 (48: 50: 54: 56: 60) sts.
Change to 9mm (US 13) needles.
Now work in patt as follows:
Row 1 (RS): P1 (0: 1: 1: 0: 0), (K1, P1) 2 (3: 3: 4: 5: 6) times, (P1, Tw2L, Tw2R, P1, K2, yfwd, sl 1, K1, psso) 3 times, P1, Tw2L, Tw2R, P1, (P1, K1) 2 (3: 3: 4: 5: 6) times, P1 (0: 1: 1: 0: 0).
Row 2: P1 (0: 1: 1: 0: 0), (K1, P1) 2 (3: 3: 4: 5: 6) times, (K1, P4, K1, P2, yrn, P2tog) 3 times, K1, P4, K1, (P1, K1) 2 (3: 3: 4: 5: 6) times, P1 (0: 1: 1: 0: 0).
Row 3: P1 (0: 1: 1: 0: 0), (K1, P1) 2 (3: 3: 4: 5: 6) times, (P1, Tw2R, Tw2L, P1, K2, yfwd, sl 1, K1, psso) 3 times, P1, Tw2R, Tw2L, P1, (P1, K1) 2 (3: 3: 4: 5: 6) times, P1 (0: 1: 1: 0: 0).
Row 4: As row 2.
These 4 rows form patt.
Keeping patt correct throughout, cont as follows:
Work 2 rows, ending with a WS row.
Dec 1 st at each end of next and foll 8th row. 42 (44: 46: 50: 52: 56) sts.
Work 11 rows, ending with a WS row.
Inc 1 st at each end of next and foll 10th row, taking inc sts into moss st.
46 (48: 50: 54: 56: 60) sts.
Cont straight until back measures 37 (37: 38: 38: 38: 38) cm, ending with a WS row.

Shape armholes
Keeping patt correct, cast off 3 sts at beg of next 2 rows. 40 (42: 44: 48: 50: 54) sts.
Dec 1 st at each end of next 1 (1: 1: 3: 3: 3) rows, then on foll 0 (1: 1: 1: 1: 3) alt rows. 38 (38: 40: 40: 42: 42) sts.
Cont straight until armhole measures 18 (19: 19: 20: 21: 22) cm, ending with a WS row.

Shape shoulders and back neck
Next row (RS): Cast off 5 sts (see pattern note), patt until there are 9 (9: 10: 9: 10: 10) sts on right needle and turn, leaving rem sts on a holder.
Work each side of neck separately.
Cast off 4 sts at beg of next row.
Cast off rem 5 (5: 6: 5: 6: 6) sts.
With RS facing, rejoin yarn to rem sts, cast off centre 10 (10: 10: 12: 12: 12) sts, patt to end.
Complete to match first side, reversing shapings.

LEFT FRONT
Cast on 24 (25: 26: 28: 29: 31) sts using 8mm (US 11) needles.
Row 1 (RS): K0 (1: 0: 0: 1: 1), *P1, K1, rep from * to last 6 sts, P1, K5.
Row 2: K7, *P1, K1, rep from * to last 1 (0: 1: 1: 0: 0) st, P1 (0: 1: 1: 0: 0).
These 2 rows set the sts – front opening edge 5 sts in g st, side sts in moss st and 1 st in rev st st between.
Cont as set for a further 3 rows, ending with a **RS** row.
Row 6 (WS): Patt 7 sts, inc in next st, moss st 8 sts, inc in next st, moss st 7 (8: 9: 11: 12: 14) sts. 26 (27: 28: 30: 31: 33) sts.
Change to 9mm (US 13) needles.
Now work in patt as follows:
Row 1 (RS): P1 (0: 1: 1: 0: 0), (K1, P1) 2 (3: 3: 4: 5: 6) times, P1, Tw2L, Tw2R, P1, K2, yfwd, sl 1, K1, psso, P1, Tw2L, Tw2R, P1, K5.
Row 2: K6, P4, K1, P2, yrn, P2tog, K1, P4, K1, (P1, K1) 2 (3: 3: 4: 5: 6) times, P1 (0: 1: 1: 0: 0).
Row 3: P1 (0: 1: 1: 0: 0), (K1, P1) 2 (3: 3: 4: 5: 6) times, P1, Tw2R, Tw2L, P1, K2, yfwd, sl 1, K1, psso, P1, Tw2R, Tw2L, P1, K5.
Row 4: As row 2.
These 4 rows set the sts for rest of left front – front opening edge 5 sts still in g st with all other sts now worked in patt.
Keeping sts correct as now set throughout, cont as follows:
Work 2 rows, ending with a WS row.
Dec 1 st at beg of next and foll 8th row. 24 (25: 26: 28: 29: 31) sts.
Work 11 rows, ending with a WS row.
Inc 1 st at beg of next and foll 10th row, taking inc sts into moss st. 26 (27: 28: 30: 31: 33) sts.

Cont straight until left front matches back to start of armhole shaping, ending with a WS row.
Shape armhole
Keeping patt correct, cast off 3 sts at beg of next row. 23 (24: 25: 27: 28: 30) sts.
Work 1 row.
Dec 1 st at armhole edge of next 1 (1: 1: 3: 3: 3) rows, then on foll 0 (1: 1: 1: 1: 3) alt rows. 22 (22: 23: 23: 24: 24) sts.
Cont straight until 12 (12: 12: 14: 14: 14) rows less have been worked than on back to start of shoulder shaping, ending with a WS row.
Shape front neck
Next row (RS): Patt 15 (15: 16: 16: 17: 17) sts and turn, leaving rem 7 sts on a holder (for neckband).
Keeping patt correct, dec 1 st at neck edge of next 2 rows, then on foll 3 (3: 3: 4: 4: 4) alt rows. 10 (10: 11: 10: 11: 11) sts.
Work 3 rows, ending with a WS row.
Shape shoulder
Cast off 5 sts at beg of next row (see pattern note). Work 1 row.
Cast off rem 5 (5: 6: 5: 6: 6) sts.
Mark positions for 7 buttons along left front opening edge – first button to come level with row 7, last button to come level with start of front neck shaping, and rem 5 buttons evenly spaced between.

RIGHT FRONT
Cast on 24 (25: 26: 28: 29: 31) sts using 8mm (US 11) needles.
Row 1 (RS): K5, *P1, K1, rep from * to last 1 (0: 1: 1: 0: 0) st, P1 (0: 1: 1: 0: 0).
Row 2: K0 (1: 0: 0: 1: 1), *P1, K1, rep from * to last 6 sts, K6.
These 2 rows set the sts – front opening edge 5 sts in g st, side sts in moss st and 1 st in rev st st between.
Cont as set for a further 3 rows, ending with a RS row.
Row 6 (WS): Moss st 6 (7: 8: 10: 11: 13) sts, inc in next st, moss st 8 sts, inc in next st, patt 8 sts. 26 (27: 28: 30: 31: 33) sts.
Change to 9mm (US 13) needles.
Now work in patt as follows:
Row 1 (RS): K1, K2tog, yfwd (to make first buttonhole), K2, P1, Tw2L, Tw2R, P1, K2, yfwd, sl 1, K1, psso, P1, Tw2L, Tw2R, P1, (P1, K1) 2 (3: 3: 4: 5: 6) times, P1 (0: 1: 1: 0: 0).
Making a further 5 buttonholes in this way to correspond with positions marked on left front for buttons and noting that no further reference will be made to buttonholes, cont as follows:

Row 2: P1 (0: 1: 1: 0: 0), (K1, P1) 2 (3: 3: 4: 5: 6) times, K1, P4, K1, P2, yrn, P2tog, K1, P4, K6.
Row 3: K5, P1, Tw2R, Tw2L, P1, K2, yfwd, sl 1, K1, psso, P1, Tw2R, Tw2L, P1, (P1, K1) 2 (3: 3: 4: 5: 6) times, P1 (0: 1: 1: 0: 0).
Row 4: As row 2.
These 4 rows set the sts for rest of right front – front opening edge 5 sts still in g st with all other sts now worked in patt.
Complete to match left front, reversing shapings and working first row of neck shaping as follows:
Shape front neck
Next row (RS): K1, K2tog, yfwd (to make 7th buttonhole), K2, patt 2 sts and slip these 7 sts onto a holder (for neckband), patt to end. 15 (15: 16: 16: 17: 17) sts.

SLEEVES (both alike)
Cast on 21 (21: 23: 23: 25: 25) sts using 8mm (US 11) needles.
Row 1 (RS): K1 (1: 0: 0: 1: 1), *P1, K1, rep from * to last 0 (0: 1: 1: 0: 0) st, P0 (0: 1: 1: 0: 0).
Row 2: As row 1.
These 2 rows form moss st.
Work in moss st for a further 3 rows, ending with a RS row.
Row 6 (WS): Moss st 6 (6: 7: 7: 8: 8) sts, inc in next st, (moss st 3 sts, inc in next st) twice, moss st 6 (6: 7: 7: 8: 8) sts. 24 (24: 26: 26: 28: 28) sts.
Change to 9mm (US 13) needles.
Now work in patt as follows:
Row 1 (RS): Moss st 4 (4: 5: 5: 6: 6) sts, P1, Tw2L, Tw2R, P1, K2, yfwd, sl 1, K1, psso, P1, Tw2L, Tw2R, P1, moss st 4 (4: 5: 5: 6: 6) sts.
Row 2: Moss st 4 (4: 5: 5: 6: 6) sts, K1, P4, K1, P2, yrn, P2tog, K1, P4, K1, moss st 4 (4: 5: 5: 6: 6) sts.
Row 3: Inc in first st, moss st 3 (3: 4: 4: 5: 5) sts, P1, Tw2R, Tw2L, P1, K2, yfwd, sl 1, K1, psso, P1, Tw2R, Tw2L, P1, moss st 3 (3: 4: 4: 5: 5) sts, inc in last st. 26 (26: 28: 28: 30: 30) sts.
Row 4: Moss st 5 (5: 6: 6: 7: 7) sts, K1, P4, K1, P2, yrn, P2tog, K1, P4, K1, moss st 5 (5: 6: 6: 7: 7) sts.
These 4 rows form patt and start sleeve shaping.
Keeping patt correct throughout, cont as follows:
Inc 1 st at each end of 15th (11th: 15th: 11th: 17th: 13th) and every foll 16th (12th: 16th: 12th: 18th: 14th) row to 32 (32: 32: 32: 36: 38) sts, then on every foll – (14th: 18th: 14th: –: –) row until there are – (34: 34: 36: –: –) sts, taking inc sts into moss st.
Cont straight until sleeve measures 45 (46: 47: 48: 49: 50) cm, ending with a WS row.

Shape top
Keeping patt correct, cast off 3 sts at beg of next 2 rows. 26 (28: 28: 30: 30: 32) sts.
Dec 1 st at each end of next and 1 (2: 2: 2: 2: 2) foll 4th rows, then on foll 3 (1: 1: 2: 2: 3) alt rows, then on foll 1 (3: 3: 3: 3: 3) rows, ending with a WS row.
Cast off rem 14 sts (see pattern note).

MAKING UP
Press all pieces with a warm iron over a damp cloth.
Join both shoulder seams using back stitch or mattress stitch if preferred.
Neckband
With RS facing and using 8mm (US 11) needles, slip 7 sts on right front holder onto right needle, rejoin yarn and pick up and knit 11 (11: 11: 13: 13: 13) sts up right side of neck, 18 (18: 18: 20: 20: 20) sts from back, and 11 (11: 11: 13: 13: 13) sts down left side of neck, then patt across 7 sts on left front holder. 54 (54: 54: 60: 60: 60) sts.
Work in g st for 4 rows, ending with a RS row.
Cast off knitwise (on **WS**).
Join side seams. Join sleeve seams. Insert sleeves into armholes. Sew on buttons.

43 (45.5: 48: 50.5: 53: 57) cm
17 (18: 19: 20: 21: 22½) in

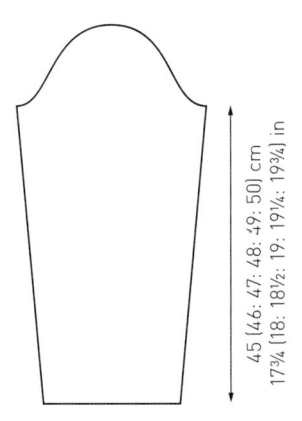

55 (56: 57: 58: 59: 60) cm
21½ (22: 22½: 22¾: 23¼: 23½) in

45 (46: 47: 48: 49: 50) cm
17¾ (18: 18½: 19: 19¼: 19¾) in

ISLA
Cosy understated sweater with frothy trims

Recommendation
Suitable for the knitter with a little experience
Please see pages 52, 53 & 55 for photographs.

	XS	S	M	L	XL	XXL	
To fit bust	81	86	91	97	102	109	cm
	32	34	36	38	40	43	in

Rowan Kidsilk Haze and Fine Lace
Kidsilk Haze
 6 6 7 7 8 8 x 25gm
Fine Lace
 3 3 3 4 4 4 x 50gm

Photographed in Kidsilk Haze in White with Fine Lace in Noir

Needles
1 pair 3¼mm (no 10) (US 3) needles
1 pair 4mm (no 8) (US 6) needles

Tension
20 sts and 30 rows to 10 cm measured over stocking stitch using 4mm (US 6) needles and one strand each of Kidsilk Haze and Fine Lace held together.

Special note: We found it preferable to knit the two yarns together from separate balls rather than winding them together.

BACK
Cast on 103 (107: 113: 117: 123: 131) sts using 3¼mm (US 3) needles and one strand each of Kidsilk Haze and Fine Lace held together.
Row 1 (RS): P1, *K1, P1, rep from * to end.
Row 2: K1, *P1, K1, rep from * to end.
These 2 rows form rib.
Work in rib for a further 22 rows, ending with a WS row.
Change to 4mm (US 6) needles.
Beg with a K row, work in st st throughout as follows:
Cont straight until back measures 40 (40: 41: 41: 41: 41) cm, ending with a WS row.
Place markers at both ends of last row (to denote base of armhole openings).
Work 6 rows, ending with a WS row.
Next row (RS): K5, yfwd (to inc 1 st), K to last 5 sts, yfwd (to inc 1 st), K5.
Working all increases as set by last row, inc 1 st at each end of 10th (12th: 12th: 12th: 12th: 12th) and 4 (4: 4: 3: 2: 0) foll 12th rows, then on 0 (0: 0: 1: 2: 4) foll 14th rows.
115 (119: 125: 129: 135: 143) sts.
Work 11 (11: 11: 13: 13: 13) rows, ending with a WS row.
Shape shoulders
Cast off 7 (7: 7: 8: 8: 9) sts at beg of next 6 (6: 2: 6: 4: 6) rows, then – (-: 8: -: 9: -) sts at beg of foll – (-: 4: -: 2: -) rows.
73 (77: 79: 81: 85: 89) sts.
Shape back neck
Next row (RS): Cast off 7 (7: 8: 8: 9: 10) sts, K until there are 11 (12: 12: 12: 13: 14) sts on right needle and turn, leaving rem sts on a holder.
Work each side of neck separately.
Cast off 4 sts at beg of next row.
Cast off rem 7 (8: 8: 8: 9: 10) sts.
With RS facing, rejoin yarns to rem sts, cast off centre 37 (39: 39: 41: 41: 41) sts, K to end.
Complete to match first side, reversing shapings.

FRONT
Work as given for back until 8 (8: 8: 10: 10: 10) rows less have been worked than on back to start of shoulder shaping, ending with a WS row.

Shape front neck
Next row (RS): K43 (44: 47: 49: 52: 56) and turn, leaving rem sts on a holder.
Work each side of neck separately.
Dec 1 st at neck edge of next 6 rows, then on foll 0 (0: 0: 1: 1: 1) alt row.
37 (38: 41: 42: 45: 49) sts.
Work 1 row, ending with a WS row.
Shape shoulder
Cast off 7 (7: 7: 8: 8: 9) sts at beg of next and foll 3 (3: 0: 3: 1: 2) alt rows, then – (-: 8: -: 9: 10) sts at beg of foll – (-: 3: -: 2: 1) alt rows **and at same time** dec 1 st at neck edge of next and foll 4th row.
Work 1 row.
Cast off rem 7 (8: 8: 8: 9: 10) sts.
With RS facing, rejoin yarns to rem sts, cast off centre 29 (31: 31: 31: 31: 31) sts, K to end.
Complete to match first side, reversing shapings.

SLEEVES (both alike)
Cast on 102 (106: 110: 114: 118: 122) sts using 3¼mm (US 3) needles and Kidsilk Haze DOUBLE.
Row 1 (RS): *K2tog, rep from * to end.
51 (53: 55: 57: 59: 61) sts.
Break off one strand of Kidsilk Haze and join in **Fine Lace**.
Using one strand each of Kidsilk Haze and Fine Lace held together throughout, cont as follows:
Beg with row 2, work in rib as given for back for 7 cm, ending with a WS row.
Change to 4mm (US 6) needles.
Beg with a K row, work in st st throughout as follows:
Work 2 rows, ending with a WS row.
Next row (RS): K3, yfwd (to inc 1 st), K to last 3 sts, yfwd (to inc 1 st), K3.
Working all increases as set by last row, inc 1 st at each end of 8th and 2 foll 8th rows, then on 11 (11: 14: 14: 13: 13) foll 6th rows, then on 6 (7: 3: 4: 6: 7) foll 4th rows.
93 (97: 97: 101: 105: 109) sts.
Work 5 rows, ending with a WS row.
Cast off **loosely**.

MAKING UP
Press all pieces with a warm iron over a damp cloth.

Continued on next page...

FEN
Chunky cabled beret

Recommendation
Suitable for the knitter with a little experience
Please see pages 16 & 17 for photographs.

Rowan Big Wool
2 x 100gm
Photographed in Smoky

Needles
1 pair 8mm (no 0) (US 11) needles
1 pair 9mm (no 00) (US 13) needles

Tension
10 sts and 14 rows to 10 cm measured over stocking stitch using 9mm (US 13) needles.

Special abbreviations
Tw2L = K into back of second st on left needle, then K first st and slip both sts off left needle together; **Tw2R** = K into front of second st on left needle, then K first st and slip both sts off left needle together.

BERET
Cast on 49 sts using 8mm (US 11) needles.
Row 1 (RS): P1, *K1 tbl, P1, rep from * to end.
Row 2: K1, *P1, K1, rep from * to end.
These 2 rows form rib.
Work in rib for a further 3 rows, ending with a **RS** row.
Row 6 (WS): K1, (P1, inc in next st, P1, K1) 11 times, (P1, inc in next st) twice. 62 sts.
Change to 9mm (US 13) needles.
Now work in patt as follows:
Row 7 (RS): P1, (P1, Tw2L, Tw2R) 12 times, P1.
Row 8: K1, (P4, K1) 12 times, K1.
Row 9: P1, (P1, M1P, Tw2R, Tw2L) 12 times, P1. 74 sts.
Row 10: K1, (P4, K2) 12 times, K1.
Row 11: P1, (P2, Tw2L, Tw2R) 12 times, P1.
Row 12: As row 10.
Row 13: P1, (P2, M1P, Tw2R, Tw2L) 12 times, P1. 86 sts.
Row 14: K1, (P4, K3) 12 times, K1.
Row 15: P1, (P3, Tw2L, Tw2R) 12 times, P1.
Row 16: As row 14.
Row 17: P1, (P3, Tw2R, Tw2L) 12 times, P1.
Rows 14 to 17 form patt.
Cont in patt for a further 7 rows, ending with a WS row.
Row 25 (RS): P1, (P1, P2tog, Tw2L, Tw2R) 12 times, P1. 74 sts.
Work 1 row.
Row 27: P1, (P2, Tw2L, Tw2R) 12 times, P1.
Work 1 row.
Row 29: P1, (P2tog, Tw2L, Tw2R) 12 times, P1. 62 sts.
Work 1 row.
Row 31: P1, (P1, K2tog tbl, K2tog) 12 times, P1. 38 sts.
Row 32: K1, (P2tog, K1) 12 times, K1. 26 sts.
Row 33: P1, (K2tog) 12 times, P1. 14 sts.
Break yarn and thread through rem 14 sts.
Pull up tight and fasten off securely.
Sew back seam.

ISLA – *Continued from previous page.*

Join right shoulder seam using back stitch or mattress stitch if preferred.

Neckband
With RS facing, using 3¼mm (US 3) needles and one strand each of Kidsilk Haze and Fine Lace held together, pick up and knit 17 (17: 17: 19: 19: 19) sts down left side of front neck, 29 (31: 31: 31: 31: 31) sts from front, 17 (17: 17: 19: 19: 19) sts up right side of front neck, and 46 (48: 48: 50: 50: 50) sts from back. 109 (113: 113: 119: 119: 119) sts.
Beg with row 2, work in rib as given for back for 7 rows, ending with a WS row.
Break off Fine Lace and join in second strand of Kidsilk Haze.
Next row (RS): Using Kidsilk Haze DOUBLE *K1, yfwd, rep from * to last st, K1.
217 (225: 225: 237: 237: 237) sts.
Cast off **loosely** knitwise (on **WS**).
Join left shoulder and neckband seam. Sew straight cast-off edge of sleeves to back and front between markers. Join side and sleeve seams.

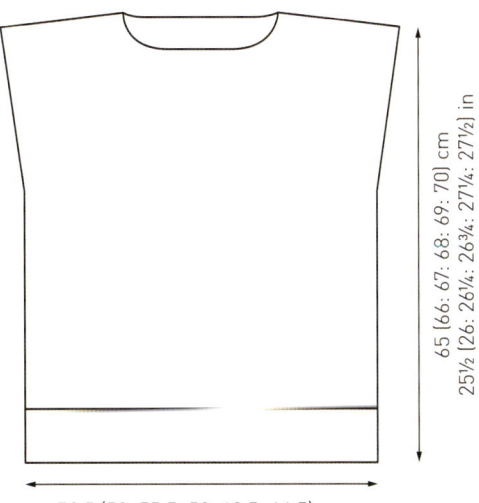

50.5 (53: 55.5: 58: 60.5: 64.5) cm
20 (21: 22: 23: 24: 25¼) in

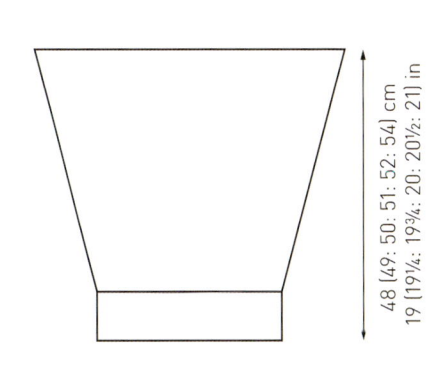

65 (66: 67: 68: 69: 70) cm
25½ (26: 26¼: 26¾: 27¼: 27½) in

48 (49: 50: 51: 52: 54) cm
19 (19¼: 19¾: 20: 20½: 21) in

INFORMATION
A guide to assist with techniques & finishing touches

TENSION
Achieving the correct tension has to be one of the most important elements in producing a beautiful, well fitting knitted garment. The tension controls the size and shape of your finished piece and any variation to either stitches or rows, however slight, will affect your work and change the fit completely. To avoid any disappointment, we would always recommend that you knit a tension square in the yarn and stitch given in the pattern, working perhaps four or five more stitches and rows than those given in the tension note. When counting the tension, place your knitting on a flat surface and mark out a 10cm square with pins. Count the stitches between the pins. If you have too many stitches to 10cm your knitting it too tight, try again using thicker needles, if you have too few stitches to 10cm your knitting is too loose, so try again using finer needles.
Please note, if you are unable to achieve the correct stitches and rows required, the stitches are more crucial as many patterns are knitted to length.
Keep an eye on your tension during knitting, especially if you're going back to work which has been put to one side for any length of time.

SIZING
The instructions are given for the smallest size. Where they vary, work the figures in brackets for the larger sizes. One set of figures refers to all sizes. The size diagram with each pattern will help you decide which size to knit. The measurements given on the size diagram are the actual size your garment should be when completed.
Measurements will vary from design to design because the necessary ease allowances have been made in each pattern to give your garment the correct fit, i.e. a loose fitting garment will be several cm wider than a neat fitted one, a snug fitting garment may have no ease at all.

WRAP STITCH
A wrap stitch is used to eliminate the hole created when using the short row shaping method. Work to the position on the row indicated in the pattern, wrap the next st (by slipping next st onto right needle, taking yarn to opposite side of work between needles and then slipping same st back onto left needle – on foll rows, K tog the loop and the wrapped st) and turn, cont from pattern.

CHART NOTE
Some of our patterns include a chart. Each square on a chart represent a stitch and each line of squares a row of knitting. When working from a chart, unless otherwise stated, read odd rows (RS) from right to left and even rows (WS) from left to right. The key alongside each chart indicates how each stitch is worked.

INTARSIA TECHNIQUE
The intarsia method of knitting produces a single thickness of fabric and is used where a colour is only required in a particular area of a row. Use short lengths of yarn for each block of colour, joining in the different colours at the appropriate point on the row. Link one colour to the next by twisting them around each other where they meet on the wrong side to avoid gaps. Ends can then be darned along the colour join lines, as each motif is completed.

FINISHING INSTRUCTIONS
It is the pressing and finishing which will transform your knitted pieces into a garment to be proud of.

Pressing
Darn in ends neatly along the selvage edge. Follow closely any special instructions given on the pattern or ball band and always take great care not to over press your work.
Block out your knitting on a pressing or ironing board, easing into shape, and unless otherwise states, press each piece using a warm iron over a damp cloth.

Tip: Attention should be given to ribs/edgings; if the garment is close fitting – steam the ribs gently so that the stitches fill out but stay elastic. Alternatively if the garment is to hang straight then steam out to the correct shape.

Tip: Take special care to press the selvages, as this will make sewing up both easier and neater.

CONSTRUCTION
Stitching together
When stitching the pieces together, remember to match areas of pattern very carefully where they meet. Use a stitch such as back stitch or mattress stitch for all main knitting seams and join all ribs and neckband with mattress stitch, unless otherwise stated.
Take extra care when stitching the edgings and collars around the back neck of a garment. They control the width of the back neck, and if too wide the garment will be ill fitting and drop off the shoulder.
Knit back neck edgings only to the length stated in the pattern, even stretching it slightly if for example, you are working in garter or horizontal rib stitch.
Stitch edgings/collars firmly into place using a back stitch seam, easing-in the back neck to fit the collar/edging rather than stretching the collar/edging to fit the back neck.

CARE INSTRUCTIONS
Yarns
Follow the care instructions printed on each individual ball band. Where different yarns are used in the same garment, follow the care instructions for the more delicate one.

Buttons
We recommend that buttons are removed if your garment is to be machine washed.

ABBREVIATIONS

K	knit
P	purl
K1b	knit 1 through back loop
st(s)	stitch(es)
inc	increas(e)(ing)
dec	decreas(e)(ing)
st st	stocking stitch (1 row K, 1 row P)
garter st	garter stitch (K every row)
beg	begin(ning)
foll	following
rem	remain(ing)
rev st st	reverse stocking stitch (1 row P, 1 row K)
rep	repeat
alt	alternate
cont	continue
patt	pattern
tog	together
mm	millimetres
cm	centimetres
in(s)	inch(es)
RS	right side
WS	wrong side
sl 1	slip one stitch
psso	pass slipped stitch over
tbl	through back of loop
M1	make one stitch by picking up horizontal loop before next stitch and knitting into back of it
M1p	make one stitch by picking up horizontal loop before next stitch and purling into back of it
yfwd	yarn forward (making a stitch)
yon	yarn over needle (making a stitch)
yrn	yarn round needle (making a stitch)-
MP	Make picot: Cast on 1 st, by inserting the right needle between the first and second stitch on left needle, take yarn round needle, bring loop through and place on left (one stitch cast on), cast off 1 st, by knitting first the loop and then the next stitch, pass the first stitch over the second (one stitch cast off).
Cn	cable needle

THANK YOU

We would like to say a huge thank you to some amazing people without whom this book would not have been possible. Graham for the fantastic photographs and editorial design, Angela for her skills on the page layouts, our gorgeous model Kristie, Diana for the great hair & make-up, Sue and Tricia for their pattern writing & checking expertise and as always – Glenis, Margaret, Alicia and Heather for all their wonderful knitting, Susan for her patience in finishing the garments, Charlotte, David, Sharon & all at Rowan. Finally, to Thelma and all at the Friends Meeting House at High Flatts for the most perfect location.

Kim, Kathleen & Lindsay

INDEX

ADAIR
DESIGN 12 & 13
PATTERN 66

ARGYLE
DESIGN 22 & 23
PATTERN 73

BARRETT
DESIGN 7, 8 & 9
PATTERN 58

BLACKENED
DESIGN 18
PATTERN 68

BREE
DESIGN 34 & 35
PATTERN 59

CECILY
DESIGN 46, 47 & 48
PATTERN 60

ELIN
DESIGN 44 & 45
PATTERN 80

EMMA
DESIGN 20 & 21
PATTERN 70

ESCAPE
DESIGN 28 & 29
PATTERN 76

ESME
DESIGN 32 & 33
PATTERN 82

FELL
DESIGN 50 & 51
PATTERN 90

FEN
DESIGN 16 & 17
PATTERN 93

GIFT
DESIGN 30 & 31
PATTERN 84

ISLA
DESIGN 52, 53 & 55
PATTERN 92

JESS
DESIGN 10 & 11
PATTERN 56

KEEPSAKE
DESIGN 24 & 25
PATTERN 69

LOVING
DESIGN 26 & 27
PATTERN 79

PALE
DESIGN 42 & 43
PATTERN 67

PITCH
DESIGN 40 & 41
PATTERN 88

SCAPE
DESIGN 37, 38 & 39
PATTERN 86

SENTIMENT
DESIGN 14 & 15
PATTERN 63

INFORMATION
TIPS & TECHNIQUES 94